# HEALING OUR IMPRISONED MINDS

## A People's Guide to Hope and Freedom

*Practical Ways to Gain Self-Understanding and Peace of Mind While Breaking the Cycles of Self-Anger, Bitterness and Resentment*

By Patrick Middleton, Ph.D.
Prisoner # AK3703 1975-

Copyright © 2004 by Patrick Middleton

*All rights reserved. No part of this book shall be reproduced or transmitted in any form or by any means, electronic, mechanical, magnetic, photographic including photocopying, recording or by any information storage and retrieval system, without prior written permission of the publisher. No patent liability is assumed with respect to the use of the information contained herein. Although every precaution has been taken in the preparation of this book, the publisher and author assume no responsibility for errors or omissions. Neither is any liability assumed for damages resulting from the use of the information contained herein.*

ISBN 0-7414-2265-4

Front cover design: Uriah Crislip
Photography: Judith Trustone

**Published by:**
**INFINITY**
PUBLISHING.COM
*1094 New DeHaven Street, Suite 100*
*West Conshohocken, PA 19428-2713*
*Info@buybooksontheweb.com*
*www.buybooksontheweb.com*
*Toll-free (877) BUY BOOK*
*Local Phone (610) 941-9999*
*Fax (610) 941-9959*

Printed in the United States of America
Printed on Recycled Paper
Published October 2004

*With profound simplicity, this book reminds us of the inherent humanity we all share--a humanity we do not forfeit even in the harshest of environments. Like the Roman philosopher emperor, Marcus Aurelius, Middleton reminds us that all exploration begins with simplicity—understanding the nature of things and using that understanding to affect change. In language stripped of hyperbole, he expresses what we all know with such startling clarity that we must take notice. This book challenges its readers to greater self-awareness while infusing them with the hope that all things remain possible."*

Fiore Pugliano, Lecturer/Advisor,<br>University of Pittsburgh

# FOREWORD

Ever since the scientific study of crime began in the nineteenth century, there have been major controversies over what causes someone to become a criminal. Social-environmental theorists, for example, believe that different racial, social, and economic factors cause individuals to turn to crime. Behavioral scientists believe that criminals are victims of drives and frustrations rooted in childhood. Then there are the biological, or genetic theorists who believe that criminality is caused by genetic or biological deficiencies. All of these theories share in common the doctrine of *Determinism*, which simply holds that we humans have little or no control over our thoughts, feelings, and actions. This doctrine says we are not the sculptors of circumstances, but, rather, the clay. But if this is true, where did such concepts as *Free Will, Personal Transformation,* and *Responsibility* come from? Simply put, they came from the human experience.

Patrick Middleton, Ph.D., is a perfect poster person for transformation. Abandoned by his biological father when he was four, he grew up in an alcoholic house with an emotionally fragile mother and an abusive step-father. Patrick spent his youth confused and angry and letting the world know about it. By the time he was 14, he was declared incorrigible and sent to live in a private home for boys. Removed from the home after he wasn't able to get along with the other boys, he bounced from children's institution to foster home and back.

When he started serving a life sentence at Western Penitentiary in 1977, after pleading guilty to robbery and second degree murder, Patrick initially channeled his anger into boxing, eventually earning his way onto the varsity boxing team where he was able to travel to other prisons for tournaments. He was also given the nickname "Rocky" by his peers and fellow boxers.

One day in the prison yard, he heard a group of prisoners called the "Frat Boys" holding a discussion on the medieval imagination. This intrigued the young lifer whose mind was always racing and curious, and it eventually led him to begin reading books. In his soon-to-be-published autobiography, he writes that it was this passage in Saul Bellow's novel *Herzog* that changed his life forever: "With one long breath, caught and held in his chest, he fought his sadness over his solitary life. 'Don't cry, you idiot! Live or die, but don't poison everything.'" These words awakened something inside him and for the first time in his life, he became aware of the workings of his own mind. He began to observe how he thought and the actions that resulted from his thinking. As he discovered ways to gain control of his battered mind, he transformed himself from a scoundrel to a scholar.

During the 70's and 80's, Western Penitentiary was the recipient of one of the most progressive prison college programs in the country. Patrick didn't waste time taking advantage of the program. With the hunger of the long-starved soul, he gulped down one course after another, earning straight A's in every course as he reconstructed a new self.

In 1983, he earned his Bachelor of Arts Degree, *summa cum laude*, and a Chancellor's Scholarship. This monetary award enabled him to begin his graduate work in the University's School of Education, where he continued to excel as a scholar. He earned his Master's in Education degree in 1984, along with another scholarship award. During his tenure as a doctoral student, he taught and lectured undergraduate students; paid room and board to the Department of Corrections out of his teaching stipends; conducted and published research reports and articles with faculty members; won several scholarships, fellowships and two teaching awards; co-authored a textbook in experimental psychology with the University's Dean of Psychology; and was the senior author of a teacher's manual and test battery for the psychology textbook.

His academic studies, along with his own healing experiences, give Patrick Middleton a unique expertise in how to find meaning and purpose for those behind bars as well as those of us living "free." His book is a roadmap for mental and emotional healing and can be used by anyone whose life is filled with suffering and despair.

Today, Patrick Middleton greets each morning with gratitude and excitement. Within the confines of the prison walls, he has created a remarkable freedom, using his disciplined and creative mind to write stories, essays, and poems. It is into this world that he invites readers to explore the riches and healing power within themselves.

As director of SageWriters.com, I have worked with hundreds of imprisoned writers over the years. This book stands alone as one that can benefit not just prisoners, but also their loved ones and the rest of us. It is truly a celebration of the human spirit.

Judith Trustone,
co-author, <u>Celling America's Soul:
Torture and Transformation in Our Prisons</u>,
Infinity 2003, and Director,
SageWriters, Box 215, Swarthmore, PA 19081
SageWriters@comcast.net

\*SageWriters.com is a community of free and imprisoned writers, artists, musicians, filmmakers, playwrights and activists working together to give an artistic voice to movements for justice, healing, reawakening compassion in our elected officials, creating a community love ethic, supporting effective re-entry programs, ending prisons as we know them and developing community-based Houses of Healing.

# ACKNOWLEDGEMENTS

### I EXALT THESE SPECIAL PEOPLE!

Three Sisters of the Immaculate Heart of Mary:
Sr. Priscilla, Sr. Rosemaron Rynn, and Sr. Patricia-Navard, who taught me reading, writing and arithmetic, and did it with so much love.

My aunts and uncles:
Millie and Perley, Ollie and Gene, Ann and Clayton, who did all they could to love and protect me.

My mother, Mary, for her unconditional love.

My sister and brothers—Suzie, Mike and Huck. Thank you for your love.

My professors at the University of Pittsburgh:
Dr. Jean Winsand, Dr. Harry Sartain, Dr. Fiore Pugliano, Mr. John Manear, Dr. Lou Pingel, Dr. Ray Garris, and Dr. Donald McBurney, who brought me books and lectures and hope by the tons.

Prisoners who taught me about friendship:
The late Brother Theodore X. Brown, Dr. Gary Gunn, Greg Lockett, Bob Hoetzel, Charlie Block and Moon StarCloud.

A sincere thanks to you, my readers. I hope so much that your life will be more meaningful and nourished by reading this book.

# TABLE OF CONTENTS

Introduction .................................................................. 1
  1) Be Honest with Yourself ..................................... 7
  2) Be Aware of What You're Thinking ................. 10
  3) Learn Simple Problem-Solving Techniques ...... 14
  4) Practice Patience ............................................... 18
  5) Work on Your Flaws Gradually ........................ 21
  6) Set Realistic Goals ............................................. 25
  7) Change Your Perspective .................................. 29
  8) Use Visual Imagery ........................................... 33
  9) Dissolve Your Bitterness ................................... 37
10) Apologize for Your Mistakes and Misdeeds ..... 40
11) Forgive Those Who Have Trespassed Against You ...... 45
12) Don't Get Sidetracked ........................................ 51
13) Live in the Present ............................................. 54
14) Reflect on All You Can Do For Yourself .......... 58
15) Take Care of Your Health .................................. 61
16) Raise Your Self-Standards ................................. 64
17) Accept Others As You Accept Yourself ........... 68
18) Expand Your Vocabulary ................................... 72
19) Don't Argue Over Trivial Things ...................... 77
20) Make the Best of Your Life ............................... 80
21) Practice Empathy ............................................... 83
22) Try a New Approach ......................................... 86
23) Develop a Support Team ................................... 91
24) Connect with Your Child ................................... 95
25) Acknowledge Your Success ............................... 99
26) Open Your Cocoon .......................................... 104
27) Kick the Gossip to the Curb ............................ 108
28) Live Every Day with a Purpose ...................... 113
29) Discover the Universal Truth .......................... 116
Selected Poems by the Author .............................. 125

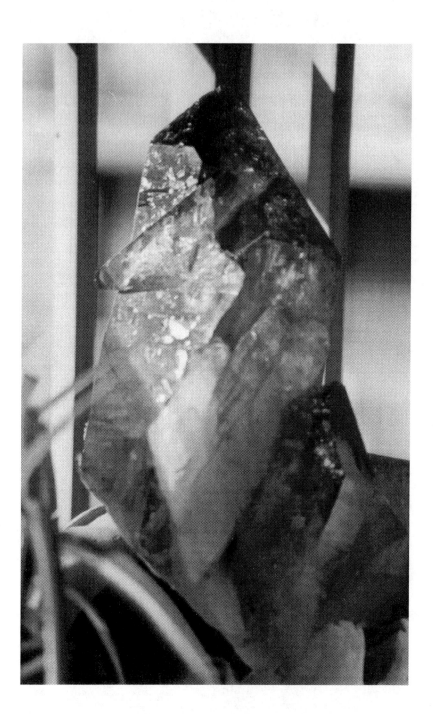

# INTRODUCTION

When people in society ask a prisoner what it's like inside, they are most often met with replies like, "It's miserable and inhumane," or "It's sheer hell." If asked to elaborate, prisoners typically point to the violence, conflicts with guards and other staff, and a lack of support from family and friends as the sources of their frustration and misery. Rarely, though, do we ever acknowledge the *real* source of our problems: a shortage of inner peace and harmony.

To put it plainly, this book is about change. If you're incarcerated and you've grown tired of being angry, resentful, and without hope, this book can help you. We start with this premise: No matter how troubled or hopeless life seems—whether you're serving ten years, fifty years, or life without parole—you can find peace of mind and a purpose for living.

We human beings are resilient creatures. We've all heard stories about someone with a spinal injury who was never supposed to walk again, but managed to do so through sheer determination and will; or the mother who was able to forgive the drunk driver who struck and killed her only child. In terms of our own life circumstances, these examples suggest that, with the right "vision" or mind-set, we can be as productive and happy as we want to be. We can become loving, generous, grateful, patient, accepting, and forgiving. And perhaps the best part of all is that when we begin to acquire more of these qualities, and any others we deem important, our lives will take on meaning beyond what we ever imagined. All it takes to begin is sincerity, determination, and practice. With these, you can learn some very simple strategies that are designed to increase your self-awareness, broaden your perspective, and keep you focused.

Despite my optimistic outlook, I don't intend to suggest that all your problems will go away, or that you won't still become confused at times. Prison is, by its very nature, an oppressive environment. There will still be times when you experience loneliness and frustration. I am suggesting, however, that whatever pain you do experience will be greatly lessened and that your problems and daily struggles can be approached with greater ease and perspective. In other words, you will have the confidence to know that you can rise above any personal crisis and get through it, and in the process, maintain your sense of well-being and dignity.

Writing this book has been fun and challenging for me. In fact, it has been one of the most fulfilling projects of my life. It's given me the opportunity to carefully reflect on what I believe to be the keys to self-redemption, peace of mind, and happiness for any incarcerated individual. While I don't consider myself to be an expert on how to find the meaning of life, I have done a pretty good job of finding happiness and meaning in my own life. As of this writing, I've been incarcerated for twenty-nine years. For twelve of those years I kept my nose pressed to the proverbial grindstone of higher learning. Between 1979 and 1990, I earned my Bachelor of Arts Degree, Master's Degree, and Ph.D. Degree, all from the University of Pittsburgh. While my areas of academic interest were as eclectic as a painter's palette, no subject fascinated me more than the workings of the human mind – particularly, how we learn and how we "unlearn." My studies in educational psychology eventually led me on a quest to find the answers to such questions as, why were the vast majority of my fellow prisoners, myself included, so miserable, so self-destructive, and so unhappy? Theories abound as to why people become criminals, and they are equally plentiful when it comes to how to bring about change. This book is not about theories. It is about practical ways to make your life more fulfilling and productive.

Obviously, there are enormous challenges in life whether one is in prison or out in society. Pain and suffering are a reality to every human being. It's interesting, though, to examine the way happy, well-adjusted people deal with frustrations, injustices, and cruelty as they go about their daily lives. First and foremost, they seem to treat themselves with respect and dignity, and they tend to possess an inner peace and calmness that radiates all around them. While they have flaws just like the rest of us, they take in stride and they are able to solve life's problems with courage, patience, and creativity.

In a weird sort of way, we prisoners are in a better position to bring about positive changes in our lives than are people in society. After all, we have an abundance of time on our hands and, thus, the opportunity to bring out the best in ourselves. The truth, of course, is that a vast majority of our days are consumed by day-to-day, moment-to-moment stuff—hassles and frustrations, disagreements, arguments, noise, chaos, and so forth. I've found that these external distractions serve one purpose only: They divert our attention away from the real source of our problems – ourselves.

My hope is that the skills and strategies presented in this book will help you begin to deal with the discontentment and unhappiness that lies within you. By embracing the very first strategy, self-honesty, you will begin to discover how to accept and nurture yourself in ways you never knew existed.

My goal is not to create a sculpture of how you ought to live your life. Rather, my hope is that the ideas in this book will help you bring about a desired change in your life for the better. As we begin our journey, my initial advice is this: Keep an open mind. The more open your mind is, the more receptive you will be to new ways of seeing. As this begins to happen, you'll experience more enthusiasm and peace of mind than you might have imagined possible. Now let's get started!

Patrick Middleton
Prisoner #AK3703
SCI-Greene
175 Progress Drive
Waynesburg, PA 15376

# DEDICATION

This book is dedicated to three people: my grandfather and hero, Mr. Ernest A. Middleton, Sr.; my mother Mary who loved me to the end; and my son and best friend, Eric "Coney" Peters.

I extend heartfelt thanks to SageWriters' Stacian Gorden, my editor and typist. A special appreciation to Judith Trustone for being a wonderful literary mentor and a trusted friend.

# 1

# BE HONEST WITH YOURSELF

Of all the characteristics that go into making a healthy, well-adjusted human being, I believe the most important one is *self-honesty*. Without self-honesty, none of us can acknowledge the ways in which we contribute to our own self-destruction and unhappiness. Self-honesty is so powerful an attribute that, combined with the genuine desire to change, one needs little else to begin the journey.

Let's begin with a test to see where you're at right now with self-honesty. I'd like you to sit or stand in front of a mirror and take a good look at yourself. *Really* look at yourself. Now as honest as you know how to be, ask yourself, "Am I happy with the person I see before me?" Take your time. Think carefully about the question. Arrive at an honest answer. If you answer yes, that you are truly happy with the person you see, then this book is probably not for you. If your answer is no, then get back in front of the mirror and ask yourself: "Who is responsible for my failures, for the condition my life is in right now?" Again, think carefully. Be as honest as you can be. If your answer to this question is any of these – society, my family, "the man," my co-defendant, and so forth, then this book probably can't help you. If your answer is, "I am mainly responsible," turn back to the mirror and ask yourself this final question: "Am I willing to work everyday for the rest of my life to change?" Think long and hard. If you answer yes, continue reading. If you are not yet sure about making such a commitment, my advice is to continue reading until you *are* sure, one way or the other.

Too often when questions like these are put to us, either in peer conversations or in group counseling sessions, denial gets in the way of honest answers. "Why shouldn't I like myself?" "I didn't put myself here." "I was framed." "I was snitched on." "I only did what I had to do to put food on the table for my kids." These are all typical responses. The truth, of course, is that they are most often simply excuses. No matter what unfair circumstances or adversities we faced in the past, there can be no doubt about one thing: We can't go back and change them. What's happened has happened. What we *can* change, though, is how we live the rest of our lives. We have choices to make.

When people are not used to being honest with themselves, it usually takes some major crisis in their lives for them to begin to face the truth. Just ask any recovering alcoholic or drug addict how they came to stop using, and they will tell you about some experience in their lives that finally led them to discover the truth about themselves and how they were living.

If you've lost your personal freedom, perhaps you are experiencing a crisis of your own. If you are reading this book, you've probably already admitted to yourself that you are not happy with the way you've been living your life and you genuinely want to change. This simple acknowledgment took honesty on your part and is the first step in the right direction.

As we proceed to the next chapter, your willingness to *reflect honestly* on the contributions you've made to your past problems and current unhappiness will go far in setting a positive emotional climate, thus opening the door for growth and progress. You can gain invaluable insights and identify solutions to problems in a fraction of the usual time when honesty is your foundation.

# 2

# BECOME AWARE OF WHAT YOU'RE THINKING

I am still amazed whenever I recall the first time I became aware of this powerful strategy. When you are able to examine your own thought processes, you put yourself in charge of your own thinking, thus empowering yourself to change the way you react to situations in your life. I believe this is the most powerful and important skill you can ever master.

Let's begin by examining the thought process in general. Thousands of thoughts travel through our minds every day. These thoughts exist in the form of ideas, desires, hopes, worries, frustrations, fears, memories, and expectations, among other things. Sometimes our thoughts are of the past, sometimes of the future. When we feel concerned or confused about something, our thoughts tell us so.

As you experience these thoughts, one of two things usually happens. First, a thought can fade away quickly. For example, I might think to myself, "I wonder if my counselor remembered to process my visitor approval form?" If I don't take it too seriously and allow it to pass by, the thought is gone as quickly as it arrived. Then the next thought pops into my mind.

The other possibility is that I hold the thought in my mind and examine it, keeping it right there in my mind's eye where I can study it and give it my undivided attention. I might think of times when my counselor was forgetful, when he assured me he was going to handle a matter on my behalf but never got around to it. Within a matter of seconds, I'm probably going to feel a little irritated. If I continue to focus on this thought, my frustration level will undoubtedly increase.

You probably already know how easy it is sometimes to get upset by practically anything. All that's required is that we give attention to something that's bothering us. The more we think about something, the more upset we become. It's just that simple. If you don't see how your own thinking contributes to the issues that frustrate you, it's always going to seem like it's someone else's fault.

When you become aware of what you're thinking, you can begin to control how you react to your thoughts. In addition, you can decide what thoughts you want to give attention to and what thoughts you want to let go. The following exercise can help you develop this awareness.

Find a time when it is relatively quiet around you, preferably when you can be alone. Get in a comfortable position, either sitting or laying down, and close your eyes. Relax. Wiggle your toes and move your ankles back and forth until your muscles are relaxed. Move each of your limbs until they're in a comfortable position for you. Be *calm*. Begin to breathe in and out slowly and deeply. Concentrate on your breathing for a couple of minutes until you've established a smooth rhythm of breathing in and out deeply. Now turn your attention to your thoughts and watch them. Let them flow freely. As your thoughts pass through your mind, your sole goal is to keep them moving. The first time you catch yourself clinging to a particular thought, tell yourself to let it go. For example, you might catch yourself thinking, "This exercise is stupid. I'm not gonna get anywhere doing this." *Let these thoughts go immediately!* Breathe in deeply and exhale slowly. If the thought comes back, counter it with something productive such as, "Wait a minute! Let me give this a chance."

At first, many thoughts will pass through your mind while you're doing this exercise, and you'll probably find it difficult to let each thought go immediately. Don't allow yourself to look in on any single one for long. The goal is to observe your thoughts coming and going as if you were a neutral bystander.

Once you are able to let go of your thoughts with relative ease, say to yourself: "I can see that I am *not* my thoughts; I am merely an observer. If I want I can let any thought pass by, or I can hold whatever thought I choose and give it my undivided attention. It's my choice."

If you spend time every day practicing this skill, your self-awareness will grow significantly. As it does, you'll become more of an *active participant* in your thinking and decision-making processes. It takes time to master this skill, so don't give up! Initially, you should devote about ten to fifteen minutes each day practicing. If you don't see immediate results in the first week, keep at it. The awareness will come.

As you become more comfortable and confident with this exercise, you can practice it while you're standing in line at the commissary or in the dining hall. The more you practice, the more you will become aware of your thoughts. With this increased awareness, you will see how you can play a more active role in the direction that your thinking — and your life -- takes.

# 3

# LEARN SIMPLE PROBLEM-SOLVING STRATEGIES

As you practice observing your thoughts and examining the way you think, you'll probably come to realize that, up until now, you haven't taken a very "active" role in your own thinking and decision-making processes. A fellow prisoner I knew for many years once put it this way when he arrived at this realization: "Up until the moment I discovered I could observe and control my thoughts, my mind had been operating on 'automatic pilot.'" When you take over the "controls" of your own thought processes, you can then begin to master the art of solving day-to-day problems constructively and efficiently.

Many years ago, I learned a simple five-step problem-solving strategy that I still use every single day. This strategy is easy to learn and you can begin to use it immediately. Here are the five steps: 1) identify the problem, 2) search for the solutions, 3) take action, 4) evaluate the effectiveness of your action, 5) try another solution, if necessary.

There are endless examples of how to use this problem-solving strategy effectively, even in scenarios that seem to have no obvious solutions. Here are a couple of examples:

Suppose you decide you've been wasting too much time hanging out with other fellows. You decide that one solution might be to stop hanging out altogether. A more compromising one might be to spend *less time* hanging out each day. Let's say you choose the latter solution and put it into effect. For the next few weeks, instead of spending four hours a day hanging out with the fellows, you spend only two. As the weeks go by, you evaluate the situation to determine if your solution is working. Hopefully, you've put your extra time every day to good use, in which case you would probably conclude that your strategy is working.

On the other hand, you may decide that you were bored stiff the entire time you were away from your friends, but you still have no desire to go back to the way things were. This raises another problem to solve: How can you spend your time more productively? Instead of giving up on the original problem, change your strategy. You might, for example, decide to spend one hour reading and one hour exercising each day. Or you may choose to engage in several different activities throughout the week, e.g., spending an hour in the library, enrolling in a self-help class, joining an aerobics group, lifting weights, etc. Whatever you decide to do with your time, as long as it's productive and you stick with it, you'll more than likely be pleased with the results.

Imagine having a cellmate who leaves his dirty clothes lying all over the floor, plays the radio loud at all hours of the day, and takes only one shower a week. Let's say you've talked to this fellow several times about these matters, but your concerns have fallen on deaf ears each time. At this point, if you're not actively thinking, you're probably ready to engage in a fight. But let's say you *are* thinking and you come up with some potential solutions: 1) you could confront the fellow one last time and tell him to change his ways or you're moving out; or 2) you could go to your counselor and ask to be moved or to have your cellmate moved. You decide that another confrontation would be a waste of time, so you vie for the latter possible solution. When you approach your counselor with the problem, she tells you that she won't be able to move you to another cell for a couple of weeks.

At this point, a common mistake you could make would be to allow frustration to knock you out of the control seat of your thought processes and conclude: "I tried, but it didn't work." On the contrary, the solution *did* work, it's just going to take a little time before it takes effect.

Rarely do our problems get solved as quickly as we would like. Therefore, we need to add patience to our list of "skills to acquire." One important thing I've learned about patience is that it's like a muscle. You truly have to exercise it to get it to grow.

When you're looking for productive solutions to your problems, you'll almost always be able to find them when you utilize the five-step problem-solving strategy presented above. No matter what the problem is, you can almost always with effort 1) identify it, 2) search for solutions, 3) take action, 4) determine if your actions are working, and 5) try another solution if necessary.

If you start practicing these problem-solving strategies right now, you'll experience immediate benefits. You'll feel less anxiety, for example, and you won't feel helpless each time you are faced with a problem. Moreover, your self-confidence will increase each time you use these steps to solve a problem. When this happens, you will have more peace of mind than you ever had before.

Remember, it takes practice and persistence to learn any new skill. The sooner you get started, the sooner you can add this one to your list of "great skills mastered." In the words of the famous Nike® commercial, "Just do it."

# 4

# PRACTICE PATIENCE

When people set out to make positive changes in their lives, the obstacle that most often prevents their success is lack of patience. Patience is defined as the ability to wait. To be patient means you exercise calmness and self-control. Generally, we are patient when we endure challenges or hardships without complaining.

I'll give you a personal example of how critical it is to learn patience. Years ago when I began to explore my inner world, I noticed a pattern to my moods. For several days, I would feel happy and excited and optimistic about my life; then, as if out of nowhere, feelings of hopelessness would rise like a fire-spitting dragon and I would suddenly become sad and discouraged. During these low periods I noticed the same disturbing thoughts occurring: "Who are you trying to kid?" "You're never going to change and you know it." "There's way too much that's gone wrong in your life for you to fix things now." Obviously, I had not yet learned how to detach myself from these negative thoughts. The more I dwelled on them, the more real they became. What I had learned, thankfully, was that it was only a matter of time before they would pass and I would be happy again, if only for a short time. All I had to do was be patient and wait.

Eventually, my investment in patience paid off again. One evening I discovered that the only thing preventing me from getting rid of my negative thoughts altogether was the attention I was giving to them. In other words, if I didn't attach significance to these thoughts, they would pass. With practice, I learned to dismiss them each time they surfaced. Eventually, I replaced them with healthy, productive thoughts.

Learning patience is absolutely critical to growth and personal development. You can't expect to change overnight, or even in a couple of months for that matter, habits and ways of thinking that you've lived with for most of your life. Meaningful change doesn't occur that way. It takes hard work and lots of practice to unlearn old habits and ways of thinking.

One of the simplest, most effective ways to develop patience is to practice the exercise you learned in chapter two – clearing your mind. Sit quietly, close your eyes, and let your thoughts go. Breathe slowly and deeply. The only focus you should have is on clearing your mind. Each time you catch yourself focusing on a particular thought, break the spell and bring your focus back to simply clearing your mind. Avoid analyzing. The goal here is simply to practice clearing your mind as many times as you need to. If you're persistent with this exercise and practice it daily, you'll begin to acquire more patience. Remember, patience is like a muscle. You have to exercise it to get it to grow. The more you practice, the more your patience will grow.

To acquire patience, it's also extremely important that you remind yourself everyday that you are human. When you make a mistake, say something inappropriate, lose your way, or simply, have a really bad day – be kind to yourself. Remind yourself that you're doing the best you can and that you need to be patient while you're learning patience. By giving yourself this gift, instead of harsh criticism, you will be building self-esteem and strength to deal with the challenges that lie ahead.

# 5

# WORK ON YOUR FLAWS GRADUALLY

At the heart of becoming a better person is the ability to accept that you're not perfect. Nobody is! Every single person has strengths and weaknesses – that's what makes us human. The important thing to understand is that we all have the ability to improve on our weaknesses and rid ourselves of many of them altogether. The key is to work on our flaws slowly. You're not going to become more patient or more loving or less angry overnight. Many of us have thirty to forty years worth of *unlearning* to do. The point to remember is, we *can* unlearn.

It took ten years for me to overcome my addiction to nicotine and other drugs. I'm still trying to stop cutting people short when I'm in a hurry. I'm also striving to be more conscious of the emotional well-being of my friends and family members and to remember that my actions affect them as well as myself. For those of us who live in a sort of emotional, self-absorbed "cocoon" in order to survive, this isn't always easy.

Let's be honest. Most of us thought we were pretty tough hombres at one time – and maybe we were. But if we examine that "toughness" honestly, we can see that it was (and sometimes still is) a front, a shield for us to hide behind. We all experience fear and anxiety and confusion inside. Part of being human is acknowledging that we have fears and worries. No matter how much work you do to improve yourself, those fears and worries will still be there to some degree. But you can take a giant step toward a healthy life when you allow yourself to admit how you're really feeling inside. Sometimes, it's risky to admit to others (your peers) that you're afraid of something or someone. It's not risky, however, to admit it to yourself; it's only humbling. When you acknowledge your fears to yourself, you're acknowledging that you're human.

Part of being human is also admitting that you have flaws. All of us do! While most of us have many flaws, we generally have two or three major ones that dominate our character – pride, machismo, jealousy, envy, bitterness, self-righteousness, impatience, greed, hatred, poor hygiene, boastfulness, laziness, and the list goes on. An integral step to becoming a more healthy-minded human being is working on your flaws.

When you begin to analyze your shortcomings, you may become overwhelmed by what you find. Some people think they're guilty of having every flaw under the sun! In their desire to be completely honest, sometimes memories of their past deeds rush forth like a raging river and give credence to the notion that: "There are so many things wrong with my character that I'll never be able to change." If you're not careful, the intensity of the experience will rob you of your enthusiasm. That's why it's important for you to take one issue at a time. Keep your expectations realistic! Don't try to work on all of your flaws at once.

If it helps, think of yourself as someone who's learning the art of boxing. You can't possibly learn the correct way to throw and land all of the various combinations of punches on your first day in the gym – or even in the first month! You have to start by learning how to jab, then how to throw a right cross, then an upper cut, and later how to bob and weave out of the way of all these punches! It takes patience and the ability to keep getting back up each time you're knocked down. When you feel yourself "falling down" (repeating a bad habit you're trying to break), get back up and start the unlearning process all over again. Use each fall as an opportunity to be kind to yourself. Don't beat yourself up when you make a mistake – learn from your experience and keep moving forward.

As an example, I have struggled with impatience for most of my life. When I made the conscious decision to work on this flaw, I also acknowledged that I needed to make better use of my time. One of my strategies in combating both was to take along a book, pamphlet, or magazine to read whenever I had to go somewhere that required waiting in line (e.g., the commissary, infirmary, dining hall, phone room). To this day, I don't go many places without taking along something to read.

When I realized that my strategy was working – by reading, I was learning patience and lots of new and interesting things --, I acknowledged my success in my journal. You see, at the time, another item on my list of "flaws to overcome" was being too critical of myself.

Acknowledging my accomplishment was another step forward for me in my goal to unlearn being overly critical of myself.

In conclusion, when you find yourself thinking too much about your flaws, back off. Use the moment to exercise patience and calm. Breathe in deeply and exhale slowly. As your thoughts slow down, your anxiety will diminish, and you'll see that whatever other flaws you have will be there for you to deal with when you're ready. Take your time. Stay focused. And, most importantly, don't be too hard on yourself!

# 6

# SET REALISTIC GOALS

For most of us, life on the outside was so crazy that, most of the time, we didn't know if we were coming or going. We were constantly nervous and anxious, and on the go. Some of us may have had worthwhile goals at times, but it's probably safe to say that most of the goals we had were centered around material things. Few of us spent time working on our inner selves, on eliminating the turmoil and confusion in our minds.

The fact that you're reading this book means that you don't want to go through the rest of your life feeling out of control and treating life as if it were a game. Wouldn't it be nice to acquire peace of mind while at the same time gain a sense of accomplishment? One of the keys to acquiring this kind of peace is to set worthwhile and realistic goals for yourself.

When you set realistic goals, you give purpose to your life and provide discipline and structure to your daily living. When you don't have structured goals, you end up living from day to day without any real purpose. During my first two years in prison I spent every day trying to distract myself from reality. My daily routine consisted of exercising in the morning, hanging out and getting stoned in the afternoons, and then going to sleep as soon as the evening count was conducted. I kept moving as fast as I could, terrified that if I stopped for a split second to ponder the seemingly endless years of incarceration and misery before me, I'd fall apart. Eventually, I was able to face my fears and come to terms with my circumstances. Since then, my life has been filled with meaning because I've never been without worthwhile goals to fulfill. The tools I used to save myself are the same ones I'm sharing with you here.

Having read this far into the book, you've probably already identified some general goals for yourself. For example, you've probably come to realize that you have the ability to change some things you don't like about yourself. You may want to be more honest and patient with yourself, more positive. Whatever your goals, you need only determination and a firm commitment to see them through.

Recently, I heard a young prisoner tell one of his friends that he didn't have time to come to the yard because he was studying for his GED exam. I smiled as I listened to the pride and determination in his voice. Here was a young buck with a solid plan, a goal to earn his high school diploma! And he had just the right discipline and attitude to succeed.

One of the secrets of such success is to set realistic goals. If you're working on your GED, for example, it wouldn't be very realistic to make your goal earning a perfect test score. To do *well* in your strongest subjects would be a more realistic goal. This is important! If you set your expectations beyond reach, you set yourself up for a major disappointment.

When I entered the University of Pittsburgh's prison college program back in 1979, my goal was simply to complete the writing course I was enrolled in. After meeting this goal, I enrolled in two courses the next semester and I set a second goal for myself – to earn A's in each course. After completing my first year of college, I set a broader goal – to earn my college degree. This gave my life focus for the next four years!

Keep your goals simple at first. Meeting your smaller goals will give you the confidence you'll need to tackle larger, more challenging goals. We call meeting our smaller goals "little victories." After all, we need to win the smaller battles before we can take on the larger ones.

Try this exercise to get started. First, write one of your goals on a piece of paper. Read it and ask yourself if your goal is clear to you. You may need to be more specific. If your goal is too broad, you'll need to narrow it. For example, let's say your goal is to be completely at peace six months from now. Right away you should know that this goal is not only too broad, but it's also very unrealistic. So how can we improve on it? Try this: "My goal is to be more at peace with issues that I have no control over." Now you have a more reasonable and obtainable goal. You can even take it down another notch by identifying what those specific issues are. One issue, for example, that you have no control over might be, "Is my wife (or husband) going to leave me?" Another might be, "How long is it going to take before it's my turn to begin stress and anger, or drug and alcohol awareness?" These issues are both out of your control!

Once your goals are clarified, you need to decide what steps and actions you're going to take in order to reach them. You'll also need to provide a time frame for completion. Again, write everything down and be specific. Make this final step fun and challenging. Be creative!

When you begin to set and meet realistic goals for yourself, I guarantee that your life will take on meaning unlike you've ever experienced. The process of fulfilling goals has a rhythm and flow. As you get into it, you'll begin to feel better about yourself and you'll gather momentum and lots of positive energy for your daily living. Start now!

# 7

# CHANGE YOUR PERSPECTIVE

So much of our experience depends on the way we see things. There's a story of two prisoners who have both been down for twenty years. A visiting official asks the first prisoner, "How do you spend your days?" The prisoner answers in a dull, lifeless voice: "It's the same old stuff every day. I get up, go to work, go to lunch, go back to work, lock up for count, eat supper, and then lock in for the night." The visitor then turns to the other prisoner and asks the same question. The second prisoner's response is quite different. In a cheerful manner, he says, "I'm a gardener. I plant all the beautiful flowers and shrubs you see around this place. Without my help, the flowers wouldn't grow."

The moral of the story is that both men are right! It's all in the way they *see* their world.

I knew a man who was once quite wealthy until he started doing cocaine. He soon lost everything he had – his wife, his freedom, and all his worldly possessions. He shared with me that being sent to prison was the best thing that could have happened to him. From his perspective, he would have ended up killing himself had he not been taken off the streets. Now he had a chance to start over and rebuild his life from the ground up, literally!

I knew another middle-aged prisoner who couldn't read a complete sentence out of the newspaper. One afternoon his wife brought their five-year old son for a visit. The child sat on his father's lap and proudly read a Dr. Seuss book out loud. When he reached the end of the book, the child turned to his father and said, "Now it's your turn to read to me, Dad." The prisoner was spared embarrassment when the guard announced that visiting hours were over. But he wasn't spared the shame he felt inside. This event, painful as it was for him, was his chance to evaluate his priorities and do something positive for himself and for the son he loved so dearly. He learned how to read.

You can take almost any situation and look at it from two sides. You can take the common path and focus on all the obstacles and difficulties, or you can take the high road and look for the hidden blessings that might be found. You can ask yourself, "What can I learn from the experience?"

Whether it's something relatively insignificant – your visit shows up late or not at all, your counselor denies your request for a new mattress, you're required to enroll in a program you feel you don't need – or something more serious – you're transferred unexpectedly to another prison, you suffer a physical problem, or you do something to wind up in the hole --, you still have a choice to make. You can find the hidden blessing, something good out of something bad.

You might be saying to yourself right now, "Take off the rose-colored glasses, Middleton." But wait! Ask yourself, "What other options do I have?" You will discover that you really only have one – you can be negative and pessimistic. You can see the situation as additional evidence that life is cruel and unfair. What kind of option is that? It might be the easier one because it doesn't require any effort or challenge, but all it does is make your situation that much more difficult to deal with. More than that, it cripples your chances of getting through the situation with dignity and some peace of mind.

Learning to change your perspective takes *practice*. You can begin by thinking of something that's frustrating you right now. Perhaps lunch was a little less palatable than breakfast, and you're frustrated because you're still hungry and your stomach is growling. Now you look at the supper menu and learn they're having liver – the meal you despise the most. (It's the meal I despise the most, too!) Now you're really frustrated. As you think about how lousy the food is, you begin to wallow in frustration. But then you remember that the way we feel depends on the way we *see*. So you decide to change your perspective. You may decide that even though you hate liver, you can still make a decent meal out of the rice and peas and carrots they're serving with it. Later, you might decide to sit down with the month's menu and circle all the really bad meals so you can plan ahead to have soup and crackers and perhaps some fruit set aside for those times. And if you really want to be creative with your thinking, you can remind yourself that you're fortunate enough not to be in prison in a third-world country where the food is considerably worse.

Obviously, reading about this strategy doesn't mean you'll always be able to change your perspective, but it's certainly consoling to know that the possibility exists.

In a beautiful poem by Robert Frost, there's a line that reads: "Two roads diverged in a wood, and I – I took the one less traveled by, and that has made all the difference." We have choices to make in every situation we encounter. To become a responsible, healthy human being, it's crucial that you make the choice to find the good in not-so-good situations. Only in doing so will you be able to come up with creative solutions and keep things in a healthy perspective. Choosing to find hidden blessings is the only way to keep bad days from being worse and difficult experiences from tearing us down. You can do it!

# 8

# USE VISUAL IMAGERY

One of my favorite songs by the Beatles is "Lucy in the Sky with Diamonds." The song begins with these words: "Picture yourself in a boat on a river, with tangerine trees and marmalade skies." Close your eyes and try to picture this scene in your mind. Is what you see in color or black and white? Do the images move or are they standing still? Can you add details to or subtract them from your picture?

If you're like most people, you've probably never really thought about the extent to which we use visual imagery in our everyday lives. When we say things like, "I can just see you now," or "Can you imagine that?" or "Just picture that," we're implying the use of visual imagery. Think about it. When we daydream or fantasize or remember some significant childhood event, we usually visualize it in our heads. If you read lots of novels or short stories, you visualize the characters and plots in order to help bring the story to life in your mind. And if you draw or paint, you probably picture the scene in your mind before you begin to create it on paper or canvas.

There are many practical ways in which visual imagery can enhance your everyday life. For starters, you can learn to visualize your goals and make them crystal clear, to "see" each detailed step you must take in order to accomplish your goals. You can use visual imagery to prepare for important meetings with your counselor or the parole board, or when you want to calm your mind, pray, or perform an exercise properly. You can also use it to make learning new vocabulary words more fun and easy. For example, let's say you're learning the word "skullduggery," which means sneaky, dishonest, behavior. Rather than just repeating the meaning over and over and "memorizing" it, add a visual image that represents the word and its meaning. My visual image of the word skullduggery involves a young boy pocketing a handful of penny candy from the counter of an old store while the clerk's back is turned. Though I learned this word fifteen years ago, whenever I come across it today, I still associate it with this image, and the meaning is right there in the image!

I recently worked with a young inmate named Jamal, who had been asked to give a speech at his upcoming high school graduation ceremony. Jamal had all sorts of neat ideas for his speech. He wanted to talk about how discovering good literature had enabled him to travel the world in his mind, about how grateful he was that he'd met a teacher who genuinely cared about his learning, and how education was the key to rehabilitation. Moreover, he wanted to be as dynamic in his presentation as Dr. Martin Luther King, Jr. had been when he spoke. A very tall order, indeed!

After Jamal had written and revised his speech, we began to rehearse his presentation. At the end of our first rehearsal, I asked him to go back to his room and visualize standing in the graduation hall looking out at the audience. When Jamal came back the next day, we added more details about the hall into his mental picture: where the clock hung, where the dignitaries would be sitting, where the band was set up, where he would place his hands on the podium, and how he would stand. We identified a particular spot on the back wall where he would focus if he began to get nervous or lose his concentration. When graduation day arrived, Jamal had pictured the details and delivery of his speech so thoroughly that, when it came time for him to begin, he was bubbling over with confidence and pride. His speech was dynamic!

It's an interesting exercise to close your eyes and focus on what you can see in your mind. If you picture a tree, for example, you can make it tall or short, fat or skinny, crooked or straight, cedar or pine, and barren or thick with leaves. You can add squirrels and robins, butterflies and snakes, and a large bee's nest. And you don't have to stop there! You can paint a blue sky or a dark sky with rolling black clouds. You can even put yourself in the fork of the tree, where you can see everything around you.

Michael Jordan was once asked how he was able to hang in the air so long before he dunked a basketball. Michael said that before he was ever able to actually do it, he visualized, over and over, doing it in his mind. Similarly, after Picabo Street's 1998 gold-medal winning race in the Super Giant slalom, Street was asked how she had managed to ski such a flawless race. She explained that the night before the race, she had gone over the course again and again in her mind, visualizing a perfect run.

Granted, you may never be the next Michael Jordan or Picabo Street, but your thoughts can certainly influence your own personal success, just as theirs did. I encourage you to practice using visual imagery everyday. You'll be amazed at how much more you'll come to appreciate your mind and all of its potential!

# 9

# DISSOLVE YOUR BITTERNESS

One day I was sitting in the library reading the jacket of a book I was about to borrow. At the table beside me, three fellows were trading stories about "injustices" that had happened to them. One man told how the cops had confiscated and pocketed several hundred dollars from him when he was arrested five years before. The same cops had beaten him at the police station and later denied the beating, he said. He was openly bitter and unable to let go of what had happened.

The second fellow complained about his ex-wife. They'd been divorced for three years, and she was given everything—the house, car, bank account, and their two kids. Ever since then he'd been trying to figure out why she left him. "I only have a couple more years to do, but she just couldn't wait. What ever happened to loyalty? What ever happened to 'stand by your man'? She wasn't any good anyway. I just know she'd better take care of my kids or she's going to answer to me."

Finally, the third guy talked about how his co-defendant had received a better deal from the D.A. and less prison time, despite the fact that the co-defendant had planned the entire crime. This guy was bitter over a criminal justice system and the "raw deal" they'd given him.

Let's keep it real. When we're frustrated most of us like to let off a little steam. Sometimes, it feels good to share our frustrations with others. And even when it doesn't feel good, sometimes we just can't help it. But there's a big difference between letting off steam every once in a while and being consumed with bitterness over things that happened in the past and that can't be changed.

When you hold on to issues from the past, when you're consumed by "unfair" things that happened to you, your heart remains filled with anger, frustration, and bitterness. When you're bitter, it's impossible for you to move on with your life.

I'm going to ask you to think of the last time when you felt really peaceful inside, no matter how short-lived it was. Maybe you had a great day, or you experienced something special. (Hopefully, you can remember such a time!) Perhaps right now you're feeling better than you have in years because you know you're getting your life on the right track; you're healing and growing. When we're feeling positive and genuinely good about something, our hearts and spirits become like a child's—filled with peace and love and good will. So where does the anger and bitterness go when you're feeling good? Simply put, it's still there waiting to raise its ugly head the second you recall the person you hold responsible for causing you bitterness. And it will *always* be there until you decide you no longer want to live with it.

Throughout my childhood and young adult life, I was consumed with anger and bitterness over my father's abandoning my family when I was five. At first I would cry whenever I thought of him. Then, I began to hold back the tears, to bite my tongue and hold in the pain. Sometimes, when I was as happy and agreeable as a child could be, something would come along that would trigger a memory of my father, and my anger and bitterness would come out. I would break things for no apparent reason, or pick fights with other children, or ride my bike recklessly into a tree. It wasn't until I was reunited with my father in 1977 that I was able to begin to let go of all that bitterness and anger I'd stored up inside me for all those years. My father and I went on to become close friends up until his passing in 2000.

The bottom line is that there's only one way to get rid of bitterness, and that is to forgive. As long as you're unable to forgive, you won't be able to move on with your life. In chapter eleven, I provide you with the tools you need in order to rid yourself, once and for all, of any bitterness you may be harboring inside you.

It's impossible to step forward with confidence and steadiness if your heart is constantly being reminded of painful things from the past, if your head is turned around looking behind. This book is about stepping forward. Instead of harboring resentment and bitterness, make the commitment to forgive and move on. Do it for yourself and your own well-being.

# 10

# APOLOGIZE FOR YOUR MISTAKES AND MISDEEDS

For some of you, this will be the most challenging chapter of your journey to inner freedom. "I'm sorry." Why are these two words so difficult for us not only to say, but to honestly *mean*? Is it too much pride? A hardened ego? An inability to reflect honestly on the past? An unwillingness to admit ever being wrong? Whatever the reason(s), if you ever want to be truly whole and healthy, expressing genuine remorse for your past actions is critical to your success.

When you say "I'm sorry" and honestly mean it, you are beginning the process of making amends for something you did that hurt someone else. You may owe an apology for something you actually did ("I'm sorry for taking your son's life") or for something you did *not* do that still resulted in hurt ("I'm sorry I didn't give you money to help support our child"). Perhaps you didn't say something you should have said to a loved one who passed away (I'm sorry for not thanking you for taking care of me when I was growing up").

The best way to make apologies is to write a list of the things you've done that have hurt others. If you have any sense that something you did hurt another person, write it down.

Plan to spend several days reflecting and writing down *all* the things you've done in your life that call for an apology. Once you've completed your list, the next step is to write a letter of apology to each person, even if they are no longer living. Some letters will be longer than others. The main goal here is to make your apologies specific and *sincere*.

Your letter of apology should be in two parts. In the first part, include specific statements of apology:

*Dear Mom* (use the name or title that best represents that person),

*I have been thinking seriously about my life and I have some things I want to share with you.*

*Mom, I apologize for . . . .*

*Mom, I apologize for . . . .*

*Mom, I apologize for . . . .*

(List as many statements of apology as you need. You'll probably list more than three apologies if you're writing to a parent.)

In the second part, include significant *feelings* statements:

*Mom, I want you to know . . . .* (Include a significant emotional statement)

*Mom, I want you to know . . . .* (Include a significant emotional statement)

*Mom, I want you to know* . . . . (Include a significant emotional statement)
(List as many feelings statements as you need).

To help you gain a clearer picture of how to write your letter, here are excerpts from my letter of apology to my grandfather, who passed away in 1975.

*Dear DaDa,*

*I have been reviewing my life recently and I have some things I want to share with you.*

*DaDa, I apologize for not spending more time with you when I came to live with you on Maple Knoll.*

*DaDa, I apologize for making you worry about me when I ran off for days at a time.*

*DaDa, I apologize for lying to you when I wrecked the car you bought me.*

*DaDa, I apologize for not coming to see you when you were in the nursing home.*

*DaDa, I want you to know how much it meant to me when you let me come and live with you.*

*DaDa, I want you to know how loved I feel each time I remember those wonderful Sundays and holidays we spent together.*

*DaDa, I want you to know how much I love you, and I want you to know how sad I've been, realizing that I was not there with you at the end of your life. I am deeply sorry.*

*DaDa, I miss you so much. I love you. Good-bye.*

Writing your letter of apology is best done by yourself, in private, and in one complete session. This is the time to let down your guard and express genuine remorse for what you've done. Some letters will flow easily from your pen. Others will be emotionally painful to write, especially when you have feelings of guilt and shame. Resist the temptation to avoid this pain. Exercise courage! Keep writing!

For your apologies to be complete, they must be expressed verbally to another person. Some apologies can be made safely to people you trust (e.g., family members with who you are in contact, your spouse, parent, child). Others should and must be made indirectly. For example, it wouldn't be appropriate to offer an unsolicited apology to a family member of someone whose life you've taken. Use good judgment when deciding which apologies are safe and appropriate to make directly to the person you have hurt.

I want to emphasize that it's *impossible* to complete the process of making a genuine apology without verbalizing your letter(s) to *someone*. The reason is that, no matter what your spiritual or religious beliefs are, your unconscious mind demands closure – and closure can only be obtained by having someone "witness" the important process you have just completed. Choose a person you trust to be your witness, even if that person isn't the person to whom you've written the letter.

A final note on forgiveness. Sometimes we ask others to forgive us. In my opinion, this request is inappropriate because when you *ask* for forgiveness, you're asking the other person to do something that you need to do yourself. This is a form of manipulation. *You're the one who needs to take the action*! Think about it. If you're asking for forgiveness, you're really trying to apologize for something you've said or done. Don't just *try*. Do it! Make an apology. Don't ask for forgiveness.

Whether it's over major offenses or small everyday things, learning to be genuinely sorry and remorseful is a critical step in the process of growing and becoming a better, healthier human being. Every time you're able to apologize and know you mean it, you'll increase your self-respect and dignity. Introduce this critical skill into your life today!

# 11

# FORGIVE THOSE WHO HAVE TRESPASSED AGAINST YOU

If we could eliminate racism, child abuse, corruption, and other social injustices from the world, it's safe to say that our prison populations would be a fraction of the size they are today. Just think about it! If the world were rid of these traumatic experiences, more children would grow up physically and emotionally healthy, leading productive lives, and the world would be a much better place.

Unfortunately, we don't live in such an ideal world. Every day children are abused and neglected in some form or fashion, and every day people are victimized because of the color of their skin, poverty, or their religious beliefs.

When you were growing up, there was no way you could have changed the actions of your parent(s), guardians, or society. Looking back on your childhood now, you can see that whatever insensitive, hurtful, or evil actions others may have committed against you happened at a time when you were helpless to prevent them. It's tragic enough that these horrible things happened to you, but it's even worse when you allow the pain you suffered to live on and control your life.

Before you can ever hope to move on and find peace of mind, it is imperative that you let go of your painful past. The longer you hold on to it, the longer it will take for you to become the loving, productive person you're capable of being. The only way to do this is to forgive those who have hurt you.

My friend Francine hadn't spoken to her mother, who had been an alcoholic for most of Francine's life, in over twenty years. "I can't forgive her for the way she neglected my siblings and me when we were kids. She doesn't deserve to be forgiven, and I just don't feel forgiveness for her. Besides, I could *never* forget some of the cruel things she did to us."

No victim of child abuse, neglect, social injustice, or a violent crime should ever be asked to forget the traumatic things that happened to them or their loved one(s). Forgetting, though, is not the same as *forgiving*. Forgiving is something we do in order to heal and move on with our lives.

By definition, forgiving means giving up the hope of a different or better past. When we openly acknowledge to ourselves that whatever happened to us will never change, no matter how hard we fight against our memories, only then are we able to begin to put the past behind us and begin the process of forgiveness.

Why should we forgive those who have trespassed against us? Aside from the fact that it's the right thing to do morally, forgiving is the *only* way to find peace of mind. When we refuse to forgive others, the resentment and anger we harbor inside eats us up like a cancer.

You can begin the process of forgiveness by making a list of the people who have wronged and hurt you in your life, even those who have died. No one is going to see this list unless you choose to share it with a spouse or close friend.

Plan to spend several days reflecting on *all* the hurtful things people have done to you for which you need to forgive them. Once you've completed your list, the next step is to write a letter of forgiveness to each one of those people, even if they have since died.

Your letter of forgiveness should be in two parts. In the first part, include specific statements of forgiveness. Then, in the second part, include significant *feelings* statements:

*Dear Dad* (use the name or title that best represents the person),

*I have been thinking seriously about my life and our relationship and I have discovered some things I want to say.*

*Dad, I forgive you for* . . . .
*Dad, I forgive you for* . . . .
*Dad, I forgive you for* . . . .

(List as many statements of forgiveness as you need).

*Dad, I want you to know* . . . . (Include a significant emotional statement)
*Dad, I want you to know* . . . . (Include a significant emotional statement)
*Dad, I want you to know* . . . . (Include a significant emotional statement)

(List as many feelings statements as you need.)

To help you gain a clear picture of how to write your letter of forgiveness, here are excerpts from my letter of forgiveness to my father, who passed away in 2000.

*Dear Dad,*

*I have been reviewing my life and our relationship and have discovered some things I want to say to you.*

*Dad, I forgive you for abandoning Mom and Mike and Suzie and me when we were little kids.*

*Dad, I forgive you for not sending me presents or calling me at Christmas or on my birthday.*

*Dad, I forgive you for not being there to take me to baseball games or to the circus or carnival when I was growing up.*

*Dad, I want you to know how much I appreciated it when you introduced me to your new family and made me feel like a son again. I want you to know how much it meant to me that you told me you loved me. Thank you.*

*Dad, I want you to know how proud I was the time you came inside the prison to see me box.*

*Dad, I want you to know how grateful I was each time you came to visit me during all these years I've been incarcerated.*

*Dad, I want you to know how sad I have been, realizing that I will never see you again. I would have loved to spend more time with you, Dad. I am sad that you didn't get to meet my beautiful and wonderful friend Ann Marie.*

*Dad, I love you, I miss you. Good-bye, Pat.*

Writing your letter of forgiveness is best done by yourself, in private, and in one complete session. This is the time to end your "relationship" with the pain by completing what is unfinished between you and the person you're addressing. This letter will help you become complete with everything about the relationship that has been unfinished for you until now. It will allow you to hold on to the fond memories and all positive aspects of the relationship you had with this person, as well as your beliefs about heaven and other spiritual principles. At the same time, you'll be able to let go of the hopes, dreams, or expectations that were not met, and of the unrealistic expectation you had of getting something from someone who couldn't or wouldn't give it.

It's important to understand that your letter of forgiveness is a private and confidential issue. Any letters you write should never be mailed or shared with anyone other than a spouse or close friend, someone you trust. Nor should you forgive someone in person. Unsolicited forgiveness is almost always perceived as an attack, and the experience may leave you feeling even more hurt and angry than before. The person(s) you are forgiving need never know that you have done so. This applies to family members, teachers, police officers, or any other authority figures who may have done you an injustice.

Even so, for your forgiveness to be complete, it's always necessary that you verbalize it to *someone* – a friend, spouse, counselor, or someone else you trust. Our unconscious minds demand closure, and closure can best be obtained by having someone witness the important process you have just completed.

The fact that you are reading this book indicates that you are searching for answers to some very serious issues in your life. Few issues are more important than learning to forgive. The information I've given you here is sound and will help you to complete unfinished business between you and others, living or dead. You have to take the first steps, though, and practice what you've just learned. Get started now.

# 12

# DON'T GET SIDE-TRACKED

Implementing this strategy isn't easy, but once you get the hang of it, you'll have the power to improve and transform your life almost instantly.

Here's an example of how it works: Leonard is walking to the dining hall. Another prisoner bumps into him and blames Leonard for being in his way. As he stands there, Leonard remembers a similar incident that happened a few months back in which a different prisoner threw a punch at Leonard. The memory leaves him feeling anxious and irritated. As a result, Leonard shoves the prisoner who bumped into him. Just as the two are ready to lock horns, a guard passes and tells them to move on. By the time Leonard returns to his cell, he's feeling confused and angry with himself. Not only did he react aggressively toward someone, but also the day before he'd picked a fight with someone else over something stupid and petty. He recalls spending the previous evening reading a book on anger management and practicing his breathing exercises. He begins to wonder if it's all worth it. He doubts that he's capable of change, and this makes him even angrier. He thinks to himself, "This is bullshit. I'm in prison. I'm not going soft. I've gotta protect myself. This place won't *let* me change."

We refer to this type of inner monologue as a "put-down attack" because that's exactly what it is – *your own thoughts putting you down*! It's difficult to overcome these attacks because, most of the time, you're not aware that they're happening. Put-down attacks usually occur when you're under stress, and they occur so quickly that you may not even realize what's happening. And that's precisely the problem! People get caught up in their thoughts in much the same way they get lost in a game of basketball or a good book. Like Leonard, most of us get side-tracked by negative thoughts from time to time. Instead of dismissing these thoughts and responding to each situation with a fresh start, we often take out our self-imposed anger on others.

Obviously, this doesn't mean you shouldn't protect yourself when you're being attacked. What it *does* mean is that our minds have a way of focusing on thoughts that feel so real and threatening that we get side-tracked from reality and blow things out of proportion.

There's a simple solution, though it's not an easy one to implement. You have to catch yourself in the midst of these tricky put-down attacks. Recognize that they're happening as they're happening. To do this, you can use the skills you learned in chapter two and observe yourself as a thinker. When you can step back and look at your thoughts, the rest is easy. Simply drop the thoughts. Dismiss them. Let them go. If it's helpful, say to yourself, "Oh, no! You're not going to fool me this time!" This will help you acknowledge that you're aware of what you're doing to yourself. The more you practice this skill, the easier it will become to catch yourself much more quickly. Rather than allowing your thoughts to control you, you'll control your thoughts. It will be *your* decision whether you think about the issue or let it go. You'll have a choice.

As you begin to gain control over your thought processes, you'll experience a great deal more peace and happiness in your daily life. Rather than paying service to your negative thoughts, you can use the energy to think about more positive things. Many men have shared with me that this has been the single most helpful skill they've acquired. I hope you'll give this strategy a fair chance – it's challenging, but it's extremely helpful. It may be the skill that changes your life!

# 13

# LIVE IN THE PRESENT

Our society is one of the most materialistic societies in the world. The philosophy that "more is better" was ingrained in our minds at an early age. It's no wonder then that we grew up wanting more and better things. As children we wanted the newest toys, the best bicycles, the latest video games, and so on. As we got older, we wanted finer clothes, expensive jewelry, a better stereo system, and a faster car. Admit it! If it wasn't these things, there were other things you wanted. And if you're anything like I was, when you got what you wanted, it wasn't long before you grew tired of it and longed for something new. New and different things would make us happy again, we thought. And maybe they did for a while, but then the whole cycle would start over. "I want. I want. I want." That was our motto!

No one is saying it's wrong to want things – that's part of human nature. The problem starts when you make a habit out of *longing for* and fantasizing about things you don't have. When this happens, you forget how to live in the present and, instead, focus on the future and the things it may or may not hold. If you stop and think about it, much of your present unhappiness is a direct result of the expectations you once had for your future – expectations that didn't come true!

It doesn't matter if you've recently arrived in prison or you've been incarcerated for years, you can help yourself enormously right now by making the commitment to let go of both the past and the future. If you can make today the focal point of your life, you will begin to experience genuine peace and tranquility inside. It isn't easy, but it's well worth the time and energy you put into it.

Living in the present means letting go of all concerns, regrets, disappointments, resentments, and bitterness from your past, as well as your expectations regarding the future. This doesn't mean you give up on your goals and dreams. It simply means you don't focus all of your attention on them. Remember what you learned in chapter seven: Change your perspective. Today should be the focal point of your life. Today should be more important to you than past mistakes or future plans.

This is a difficult strategy to implement because detaching your mind from the past and future is a subtle process. In fact, you may be so bound to the past or future that you can't relate to what it feels like to live in the present. If this is true, you'll need to work extra hard to gain this ability.

One exercise that works well is to practice using your senses. Open your eyes as wide as you can and focus on your surroundings. If you're looking at a chair, take in everything about it that you can: its size, shape, color, height, thickness, texture, etc. Your complete focus should be on that chair. If you have an apple, place it in the palm of your hand.

Observe how it feels. Is it cold or warm? Hard or soft? Small or large? Smooth or rough? Red or yellow or green? As you proceed, stop often to remind yourself that you're observing these objects in present time. Don't let your mind wander to any thoughts of the past or future. Focus on the here and now.

Next, engage your ears. Take notice, *really take notice*, of the sounds around you: flushing toilets, running water, gurgling plumbing pipes, screaming voices, the stirring wind, etc. Acknowledge that these are familiar sounds that are occurring in present time. What can you smell? Incense, mildew, deodorizer, dirty socks? Take the time to recognize these smells. Remember you're an observer. Don't allow any of your thoughts to be judgmental during these activities. Observe. Observe. Observe.

You can take that apple and bite into it. What does it taste like? Is it sweet or sour? Crunchy or mushy? Fresh or rotten? Now take your shoes and socks off. Place several items on the floor—a pencil, a piece of crumbled up paper, a shoe, a bar of soap, etc. Walk delicately across these items. What do they feel like? Which ones tickle your feet? Which ones did you have to walk gingerly over? What did it feel like to put all of your weight down on that crumbled piece of paper?

The nice thing about these exercises is that you can do them just about anywhere and anytime. When you're walking in the yard and hear the birds singing and the bees buzzing; when you're sitting in church or the mosque; when you're chewing your food in the dining hall, you can practice observing in the present.

When you do these exercises correctly, you should experience a total absence of both the past and the future. Practice a few minutes each day, and you'll see how you begin to slow down and relax more. You'll begin to free yourself of boredom, worries, and petty concerns. When you learn to live in the present, to *feel* the here and now, you'll know what peace of mind is like. You'll open the door to a whole new way of looking at life. Give yourself this gift.

# 14

# REFLECT ON ALL YOU CAN DO FOR YOURSELF

This is a strategy for regaining perspective. It doesn't take long, and if you make a real effort, it can bring powerful and lasting benefits to your life. Specifically, the strategy tackles one of the most common pitfalls we prisoners face – the feeling that there's nothing to do but time, the nagging sense that being in prison means your life has no meaning or purpose.

How many times have you heard someone say, "This place is boring," or "There's nothing to do in this joint?" You've probably even said something like this yourself. The truth is, prison can be a dull place if that's how you choose to perceive it. You can change your perspective at any time, however, if you stop and reflect on all the things you could be doing for yourself. Try it and you'll be amazed at what you find!

Dave started painting still-lifes and country scenes about five years ago. Now he's doing portraits as well as still-lifes, and he's earning money for his work! Another brother, Rafi, has been studying African American literature for all of the twenty years we've known each other. By anyone's standards, Rafi is a true literary scholar. Then there's our jailhouse poet, John Paul, who's had volumes of his poetry published. I could fill a whole book with examples of men and women prisoners who've realized their true gifts as human beings and opened their minds to their own potential.

If you think about it, there are probably things you're not doing for yourself that you know you could be doing. Are you getting enough exercise? Are you taking care of your personal hygiene? Do you read books and magazines that stimulate your brain and make you think? Do you listen to music? Do you keep your cell clean? Do you write to your loved ones? Are you practicing the strategies you're learning in this book?

If you're committed to changing your life, to developing into a healthy-minded, productive human being, you need to understand that the choices you make from now on will either contribute to your goals or hinder you from reaching them. Your growth and development and peace of mind depend on all the things you do for yourself. Here are some suggestions to help you get started:

1. Go to school or college if it's available.
2. Exercise and get in shape.
3. Write letters. (We all have fences to mend!)
4. Visit the library each week.
5. Research your own legal case. (Don't depend solely on your attorney!)
6. Enroll in a self-help course (e.g., stress and anger, parenting, A.A., N.A., or wellness education).
7. Get involved in a sport you like.

8. Take up a hobby (e.g., chess, drawing, crossword puzzles, writing, collecting pictures).
9. Read books that interest you and challenge your mind.
10. Take five dollars and start a bank account.
11. Attend weekly religious services.

And this is only the beginning! There's a host of activities and projects you can get involved in to better yourself. You simply need the willingness to put your heart and mind into it. The poet, the painter, and the literary scholar weren't born with polished skills; they worked long and hard to reach their goals. They had to do it for *themselves*.

My advice is that you avoid the temptation to focus on what you could be doing if you were "free." Instead, spend more time thinking about what you *can* do for yourself *now*—and appreciating those opportunities. If you find one positive thing to do for yourself each day, you'll feel gratitude. You'll be amazed at how your self-pity will subside, how your self-respect will grow, and how your life will take on a whole new meaning. Get with it!

# 15

# TAKE CARE OF YOUR HEALTH

I knew a prisoner named Thomas who worked in the law library for over ten years. Every day Thomas read law journals from cover to cover and gave legal advice to anyone who needed it. In the evenings, he read more law books in his cell and wrote legal briefs for himself and other prisoners. Over the years, Thomas helped several men get their cases overturned and win their freedom.

One day, the U.S. Supreme Court informed Thomas that his own legal options were finally exhausted. The news devastated him. He was so sure that his final appeal would win his freedom. Almost overnight he became depressed and bitter. He stopped reading law books and giving legal advice. After a couple of weeks, Thomas quit his job in the law library and withdrew from everyone. He became a recluse. One morning while he was lying in bed, Thomas's heart stopped beating and he died.

Sadly, Thomas's story is all too familiar to anyone who's been in prison for any length of time. I've known hundreds of men like Thomas—men who gave up on themselves and spent their days doing nothing but playing cards, watching television, listening to the radio, chasing drugs, or just sitting around reading for hours upon hours.

Neglecting your physical health is a telltale sign that you've either given up on life or just don't care enough about yourself. The fact that you're reading this book indicates that you've made a decision to change your life and live responsibly. This alone shows that you care about what happens to you and to your mental health. But that's only half of the equation!

You may already know that exercise helps to reduce stress, lower cholesterol, diminish body aches, and strengthen the heart and lungs. What you might not know is that exercise can also help combat depression and substance abuse and increase your self-esteem. When we exercise, our brain releases natural drugs called *endorphins*, which are tranquilizing and pain-killing hormones. If you're physically active, you already know how good your body feels when you're involved in vigorous activity. I'm an avid handball player. Every time I step onto the court, I look forward to the "high" my mind and body experience when I play hard.

Exercise is also renowned for its stress-busting, morale boosting powers. When you have a lot of pent-up frustration and anger, there's nothing like a good hoop game or aerobics session to take the edge off.

I just know that some of you are sitting there right now saying, "Hey, I'm not into sports or lifting weights or jogging." And that's fine. The fact is, you don't have to be into sports to take care of your physical health. There are plenty of physical activities that don't require a high level of athleticism. You can take up yoga, for example, enroll in an aerobics program, learn a regimen of calisthenics that you can perform alone in the yard or in your cell, or power walk two or three days a week. You can quit smoking, too, and change any bad eating habits you may have. A few years ago, I stopped eating most red meat, and I feel much better for having done so. At the same time, I started eating more vegetables and fruit. (Okay. I confess. I still eat way too much chocolate!)

If you're overweight or have health problems, see a doctor to discuss a diet and exercise plan that will work for you. Remember to keep your goals realistic. Losing weight and building muscle tone take time, so avoid crash diets—they put your health at risk, and they only provide temporary results. Eat smart and stay active! Your work will pay off in the end.

When you take care of your physical health at the same time you're taking care of your mental health, you can't help but feel good about yourself. You'll develop discipline while you provide a healthy structure to your day. More important, you'll be sending a message to everyone around you that you respect yourself, and that's a good thing!

# 16

# RAISE YOUR SELF-STANDARDS

We've all heard the saying that actions speak louder than words. We can take this to mean that the way we live our lives demonstrates the kind of person we are. Our strength, integrity, humility, sense of well-being, compassion, generosity, willingness to forgive, and an array of other noble qualities are, above all, the true voice of who we are.

How many times have you heard someone say, "I'm not the same person I was a year ago (or two years ago, or three)"? Perhaps you yourself have uttered these words to someone. If so, hopefully you meant them in a positive way. Whenever I hear someone make this statement, I am reminded of one of the most important choices we humans have: the choice to change for better, or worse, or remain the same. In other words, we can *choose* to raise our self-standards and *evolve*. We take the first step in this process when we begin to take responsibility for our own actions.

In 1980, I met a brother named Carl in a sociology course the two of us were enrolled in. When I first heard Carl speak, I knew he was the brightest and most articulate prisoner I'd ever met. He had what seemed like a natural ability to use simple, concrete analogies to explain complex theories. When he spoke on such topics as poverty, racism, and the causes of criminality, he didn't just point the finger; he offered viable solutions to these complex problems.

Carl's belief that education was the key to escaping poverty and a life of crime made him determined to complete his education once he was released from prison. He was, in his own words, a man on a mission—to raise his self-standards.

As Carl's release date got closer, we all reminded him of other prisoners who'd gone back to the streets with lofty goals only to abandon them once they got there. Carl was also reminded that he'd been in and out of prison all his life. Carl didn't get angry by these comments. He merely replied that he'd found his mission in life, and he was going to walk the walk, not just talk the talk. Nothing, he vowed, would stop him from continuing his education and remaining free.

Carl was true to his word. When he went home, he entered a private college and caused quite a sensation. His academic research led him to expose the school's practice of giving financial aid to the apartheid country of South Africa.

Eventually, Carl left that college for another, but he never abandoned his goals. He went on to earn his Master's Degree, and then he founded the Council for Urban Peace and Justice in Pittsburgh. In 1993, Carl organized the first national gang summit, which peacefully brought together some of this country's most notorious gangs. Recognized by President Clinton for its historic significance, the summit instantly catapulted Carl into the national spotlight. Until he passed away in the summer of 2003, Carl was lecturing at universities and conferences all over the country on the state of urban affairs. He even addressed the United Nations. His very successful and inspirational autobiography <u>Convicted in the Womb</u>, by Carl Upchurch, should be on every prisoner's reading list.

For Carl, raising his self-standards involved getting an education and moving beyond just talking the talk to "walking the walk." His life is a living testimony to what happens when human beings raise their self-standards and begin to believe in themselves. Carl remains a great inspiration to me and to many other prisoners who've known him.

Raising your self-standards might involve any number of worthwhile endeavors. A good place to begin is to look back on goals you've set in the past but later gave up on. Here's an exercise that can help you.

First, write down two or three goals you once had which you didn't see through. Once you've identified these goals, ask yourself what got in the way of your success. Perhaps you lost sight of your goals because they weren't clear enough to you. Maybe they were too broad and unattainable. Maybe you had a few bad days and simply lost your confidence and drive. Or perhaps you fell victim to one of the biggest reasons people fail to meet their goals – a lack of good planning.

Whatever the reason(s), you can renew your commitment to any goal any time you're ready. First, though, be sure you rethink each one and clarify each step you're going to take to see the goal through. Go back and read chapter six in this book and follow the steps in the goal-setting process.

Raising your self-standards, whatever they may be, will increase the quality of your life tenfold. When you focus your energy on pursuing productive and meaningful goals, something wonderful begins to happen to you. First, your self-confidence begins to grow, and you begin to acquire a certain amount of grace and humility. You become kinder, less selfish, and more at peace. Using the words from one of my favorite Beach Boys songs, others will begin to pick up "good vibrations" from you. When this happens, you can't help but feel good about yourself and want more of this feeling.

With each new change you make in your life, you'll reap immediate benefits. All of us have room for improvement, things to work on. There are no limits to this challenge.

# 17

# ACCEPT OTHERS AS YOU ACCEPT YOURSELF

We all have the ability to treat ourselves and others with respect and dignity. Yet, there are millions of people in the world who are broken, angry, hostile, and miserable. For a variety of reasons, our society and prisons are filled with people who go through life treating themselves and others with disdain and cruelty. Many others suffer from a bad case of self-importance and appear to like only themselves. And then there are those people who accept and respect both themselves and others.

The most precious gift you can give yourself and, ultimately, everyone around you is the gift of self-acceptance. When you make the conscious decision to accept and respect yourself, you're on the right path to becoming healthy and whole. There's one other factor, however, that you must consider along with accepting yourself and that is—accepting others.

The truth is, it's not possible to genuinely accept yourself and not accept others at the same time. We accept others when we embrace the ideal that all human beings deserve to be treated with respect and dignity.

Making the conscious decision to accept other human beings, regardless of their religious beliefs or skin color, doesn't mean you have to like every person you meet. It simply means that you accept and embrace the universal principle that no human being is better or worse than another. This may be one of the most difficult decisions you ever make. When you stop and think about some of the cruel things that have been done to you and others you love, it's not easy to feel that other people deserve your love and respect. Tell any victim of a hate-crime that his perpetrators deserve to be treated with dignity, and that person may just have a few choice words for you.

Sometimes our life experiences make it difficult to embrace a universal acceptance of others. But when your heart is callous and filled with hatred toward another person or group of people, your capacity to grow and mature is limited. Hatred and resentment, whether aimed at oneself or others, are like poisonous plants in a spiritual garden: Good things cannot take root and grow around them.

So, how do we stop hating and resenting others? First, you make the conscious decision to move beyond your life experiences and embrace the philosophy that the ultimate goal of all human beings is *acceptance of one another*. This requires a leap of faith. It doesn't mean you have to sit in a room singing "Kumbaya" with your enemies. What it does mean is that, if you've had a hundred or a thousand bad experiences with white people or black people or Jews or Christians or Muslims, or *prison guards*, you don't draw a sweeping generalization that *all* white people or black people or Jews or Christians or Muslims or prison guards are bad.

Second, practice acceptance of others every chance you get. When you find yourself in conflict with another person or group of people, ask yourself what exactly it is that's causing you to feel the way you do. Was it something the other person said? Or the way they said it? Or perhaps it was the way that person looked at you? Stop and remind yourself that, whatever it was, you have a choice to make: You can choose to hate the person or you can hate that person's actions and behavior. There's a big difference between these choices! In choosing the latter, you maintain your self-respect while at the same time you break the cycle of hating others.

It may help you to remember that when people treat others with hatred, they often do so out of fear and self-loathing. Their self-esteem may be so damaged that the only time they feel good is when they're making the lives of others difficult. When you learn to recognize these kinds of people, you have the power to *not respond in kind*. Fighting hatred with more hatred is like fighting fire with gasoline – it only compounds the problem. You can break this cycle by practicing tolerance and patience.

Third, practice empathy. When you see others doing some of the same irresponsible things you used to do, take a moment to recall how you used to be. Perhaps you detest it when you hear other brothers putting women down (calling them "bitches" and "ho's") when you yourself used to do the same thing. Or maybe you used to resort to nasty name-calling when someone made you angry. One of the most effective ways to practice tolerance is to put yourself in the other person's shoes, and one of the best ways to do that is to acknowledge, when it's appropriate, that you yourself once walked in those same shoes. Practicing empathy will not only increase your patience and tolerance for others' shortcomings, but it will also enhance your own self-esteem.

Fourth, be aware of peer pressure. When you're around others who are promoting hatred and meanness, tell yourself that this is unacceptable behavior for you. Never join in just to fit in. If you're not able to act positive toward or say something positive about someone, don't say anything at all. Most importantly, learn to choose friends who are positive and respectful of others.

Finally, don't lose sight of your goals. Conflicts often arise when you're around people who aren't about what you're about – changing your life for the better. When this happens, it's easy to forget for the moment the new ideals and values you're working on acquiring. To grow and mature, it's crucial that you set aside your anger and pride during these times and keep your goal of accepting others in front of you. The key is to be *vigilant* over the presence of old feelings inside of you, so that you can turn them off when they surface and not allow them to distract you from your new way of living. An incredible shift takes place when you do this. It brings forth an abundance of new happiness in your life. Try it!

# 18

# EXPAND YOUR VOCABULARY

The first book I read in prison from cover to cover was *The Autobiography of Malcolm X*. Being the slow reader I was at the time, it took me about two weeks to finish the book. When I did, I'd not only discovered the value of learning, but I'd also acquired a life-long affinity for words. Reading how words and ideas had brought so much meaning to Malcolm X's life inspired me to want to read more and to increase my vocabulary in the process.

After reading Malcolm's book, I began to collect every new word I came across in my reading. I wrote each one on the wall of my cell, using a colored, erasable marker. No sooner did I "own" one word – I understood it as well as my own name – than it came down and was replaced with another.

It's safe to say that if you're reading this book, you're hungry for knowledge, too. That's fantastic! One of the advantages of prison is that we have plenty of time on our hands to learn. It doesn't matter what your educational level is, all you need is a genuine desire to learn. Did you know that when you increase your vocabulary, you also increase your general intelligence? It's true! The more words and concepts you understand, the better thinker you become.

Another reason for increasing your vocabulary is that, no matter what subject you're dealing with, your starting point is always with words. Have you ever noticed that just about every discipline and vocation has its own unique set of words? If you're learning to read music, for example, you need to know the meaning of such words as *arpeggio, crescendo, and inversion.* If you want to be a welder, you'll need to know what *mig* and *tig* mean. (You'll also learn a whole new meaning for the word puddle.) Similarly, if you're studying poetry, you need to know what *metaphor, simile, verse, rhyme, and meter* mean. Even self-help books such as this one have a vocabulary of their own.

When you were learning new words in school, you probably relied mainly on the dictionary – you looked words up and memorized their meanings. Looking a word up in the dictionary and studying its meaning is a good place to start, but it's hardly ever a good place to end the learning process. To truly "own" a word, you need more than just the dictionary. (Owning a word means you are able to comprehend the meaning of the word when you hear someone else use it, *and* you are able to use the word appropriately in your own written or spoken communication.)

Two excellent techniques you can use to help you learn new words and information are the use of association and visual imagery. These skills make learning easier and more fun! Here's how.

*Association*. After you look up a new word in the dictionary and understand its meaning, the next thing you should do is associate the word's meaning with something you already know. Say, for example, the new word is *clandestine*. You look the word up and learn that it means "something done or kept in secret." Then you notice that the first four letters in the word sound like the word *klan*, as in Ku Klux Klan, which you know is a *secret* society of white men who are anti-Black, anti-Semitic, anti-Catholic, etc. By processing new information (the meaning of the word *clandestine*) with something you already know (*Klan*), you'll be able to easily retrieve the newly acquired information the next time you need it. When you come across the word clandestine months later, your memory will trigger the association you made previously, which will give you instant recognition of the word and its meaning.

For example, let's look at the word *empathy*. If you're not familiar with this word, you're no doubt familiar with its rhyming cousin *sympathy*. Both of these words contain the root *–pathy*, which comes from the Greek word *pathos,* meanig "to suffer or feel." When we have *sympathy* for others, we share in their pain and suffering. The word *empathy* also has to do with feeling. Having empathy for another person means we can relate to their pain and suffering. We put ourselves in their shoes (mentally) so we can understand their plight (see Chapter 21).

Perhaps you already knew the meanings of both sympathy and empathy. Here's another rhyming cousin of these two words that you may not know – *apathy*. You can use the process of association to easily connect this word to the others. The word *apathy* contains the prefix *a-*, which means, among other things, "not." (A person who is *asexual* is not sexual; one who is *apolitical* is not concerned with political matters.) A person who has apathy *(a + pathy)* for another does not feel for or suffer with them, but is indifferent and uncaring.

Using the process of association, you can link these three words together by knowing that they share the root – *pathy*, which means to feel or suffer. While you're at it, you may also want to look at other words in the *–pathy* family, such as, *pathology, pathetic, pathological, and pathos.* You may be amazed to know that all of these words are related in meaning.

<u>Visual Imagery</u>. My favorite method for learning new words is using visual imagery. When you use visual imagery to learn new words, you create a picture in your mind that represents the meaning of the word you're trying to learn. This process is fun and creative. Here are a couple of examples.

Let's start with the word *façade* and the sentence, "Every building has a façade." When you look up this word in the dictionary, you learn that it means, "the front of a building." Now close your eyes and picture yourself walking through an amusement park at night. You turn to your right and notice that the front of the building is shaped in the form of a large clown's face. This *face* is the building's *façade*.

When creating visual images, it's helpful to add bizarre and vivid details. For whatever reason, our minds recall images that are silly and bizarre faster and more precisely than they do images that are dull and ordinary. So, let's add a big red nose to our clown, eyes that blink, and a front door with a "bling-bling" diamond. Let's make his left eye the entrance to the "tunnel of fun," and the right one the exit. Now stand back and look at the façade (front) of the building. The façade is a clown's face and the face is a façade. Get it? If you do, you'll never forget the meaning of this new word, façade.

What if we use association and visual imagery together? Let's revisit the word *clandestine*. Close your eyes and picture a bunch of silly-looking men with sheets over their heads standing out in a country field late at night walking in circles. They're having a secret meeting. Say to yourself, "The Klan is having a *clandestine* meeting. A *secret* meeting of fools." Now add some details: Pick-up trucks with confederate flags hanging in the rear windows; bright orange flames on the ends of sticks stuck in the ground; black and purple clouds swirling overhead, etc. The possibilities for details are endless!

If you spend the next six months practicing visual imagery and association while learning a new word or two every week, I can almost guarantee that you'll be "hooked" on learning forever. There's only one way to grow and expand, and that's *to learn*. The gift of learning is what saved my life. It can save yours, too.

# 19

# DON'T ARGUE OVER TRIVIAL THINGS

This strategy seems like common sense, but if you think about it, most of us rarely argue over truly important things. It's the little things, trivial and unimportant, that we get bent out of shape about the most. We argue about whose turn it is to clean the cell, who drank the last cup of coffee, which judge in the county has the toughest reputation, who sold the most drugs in the neighborhood, or whether or not the next meal is worth the walk to the dining hall.

We get angry when we have to wait in line to use the telephone, when a guard shouts orders at us, or when our counselor recommends that we enroll in a program we don't think we need. I knew a man who started a fight because his cellmate watched too many "Jerry Springer" reruns! What could be more important than that?

If you could reduce the arguments you have over insignificant things, your life, and the lives of those around you, would be much better. You would save precious energy and avoid the frustration that comes with arguing, thus reducing the amount of unnecessary stress in your life. Not only that, you would avoid the potential for a situation to escalate into a physical confrontation. How many times have you seen a senseless argument turn into a fist fight?

The strategy to avoid unnecessary arguments takes some work, but it's definitely something you can learn with time and practice. The first step calls for putting things in the right perspective. Try to reflect on what is truly important to you – your family, your spiritual beliefs, your goals --, and commit to letting go of unimportant things. Ask yourself, "Do I really want to waste my life arguing everyday, or feeding into other people's arguments? Do I really want to put my peace of mind and safety in jeopardy?" By asking these questions every time you feel the urge to argue, you give yourself a reality check and a "time-out." You'll more than likely conclude that arguing is not worth your time and energy.

When you argue over little things, often you're really frustrated at something completely unrelated. This brings us to the crucial second step in your strategy: Identify what's really bothering you. Once you do that, you're in a better position to diffuse your frustration over minor things and instead deal with the *real* issues in your life.

Last winter, I learned that we were about to get a serious snowstorm in the area. Knowing that my friends from State College were planning to visit the next day, I tried to reach them by phone, but no one was home each time I called. When I returned to my cell, the search team was there to greet me. After they'd emptied out my footlocker and cabinet and had all my personal possessions strewn out across my bed and the tops of the cabinets, they left the cell.

Already frustrated over not being able to reach my friends on the phone, I was just about ready to chastise the guards when it suddenly occurred to me – thankfully – that they hadn't broken or taken anything. I could easily put things back the way they were. I realized that arguing with them would get me nowhere. I knew, too, that the real source of my frustration was in not being able to reach my friends.

Later that evening, I called my friends and they were at home. They assured me they would call their AAA office in the morning to check on road conditions before they started out on the one hundred and forty mile drive. Everything turned out fine!

It's so much more comfortable to be around people who aren't always frustrated and picking arguments. Whether or not you wish to see yourself as a role model, when you refuse to argue over trivial things, you set a good example for others. When you're patient and calm, you become someone others want to be around. Your sense of humor unfolds, and people notice you.

I can't stress enough how much more at peace and healthy you'll be when you apply this strategy to your life. From now on, when you find yourself arguing with another person, *stop*. Just stop. Think about what it is you're arguing about and ask yourself if it's important. Try to pinpoint what it is you're really angry about, and you'll be able to put things into the right perspective. This will take some reflection and the willingness to change a few habits, but it's well worth the effort.

# 20

# MAKE THE BEST OF YOUR LIFE

If you ask any prisoner the one thing he or she wants the most, the answer would most likely be *freedom*. Over the years, I've heard so many men say, "If only I were out there now, I wouldn't have to put up with all this noise and bickering and other crap." While this may be true, it's also true that you'd definitely have to put up with something else. There's no way around it. Whether it be a parole officer monitoring your activities, bills that need to be paid and not enough money to pay them, the pressure to find a better job, or some other problem – you would definitely have to put up with some "crap" on the outside.

Would it still be better than being incarcerated? Of course! Any sane person would prefer to be just about *anywhere* than locked inside a prison. But when you focus on where you'd rather be instead of where you are, or you compare what you have (or don't have) to the fantasy of having something else, all you're doing is bringing a great deal of unnecessary stress and frustration upon yourself.

More importantly, you're preventing your life from being all that it can be *right* now. The fact is, you're in prison, not on the street. You can *choose* to dwell on wanting to be some place else, or you can make the best of your present situation.

Wanting what you don't have is hardly something only prisoners do. A close friend of mine out in society works with very fortunate people every day – people who earn a lot of money, who have beautiful homes, who work in positions of considerable power – and these people too fall prey to the "if only" trap: "If only I had a bigger office." "If only I could make more money." "If only I had a better set of golf clubs."

It sounds shallow, and it is! Here are "free" people who seem to have everything in life, yet they want more, something else, something different. I use this example to point out that it isn't what we *have* in life that determines our peace of mind and happiness – it's what we are on the inside.

To feel peaceful and satisfied in your life, you first need to break the "if only" habit – if only you had your freedom, or your girlfriend back, or a better job, etc. These thoughts are nothing but distractions. Try something a little more creative – *live in the present.* Try to structure your daily living around the work you're doing to improve your life. Make learning the skills in this book the major priority in your life.

I'd like to think that you've reached a point in your life where you realize that you, and only you, are responsible for your own peace of mind. Congratulations! To truly want to grow and develop and become the whole person you know you can be takes courage and a lot of inner strength. It's important that you acknowledge you're doing the right thing for yourself, perhaps for the first time in your life. This is a blessing! Cherish it!

# 21

# PRACTICE EMPATHY

At some point in our lives, we've all felt compassion and sorrow for another person – be it a friend who lost a family member, a dying child we knew or read about, a homeless person we passed on the street, or any number of other situations. It's been said that the more capable we are of feeling compassion for others, the more human we are.

Equally important in making us more human is the ability to experience *empathy* for others – to understand and relate to someone else's pain and suffering. Learning to empathize is a critical step in the process of becoming a mature, healthy-minded person. Without practicing empathy, we remain indifferent, self-centered, alienated from others, and doomed to repeated failures.

A young prisoner named Troy stood up in a wellness educations class I once attended and said: "The kid I shot? I know now what his mother's going through. I saw my mother get killed when I was 14. It was the worst day of my life, man. My mother was my best friend. We did everything together. We used to go shopping all the time for clothes and CDs. We went to Sixers' games together. She was my whole world. Maybe that boy I killed was like that with his mom, and now she doesn't have him anymore. It's sad." Standing there, Troy was outwardly shaken and remorseful.

Fortunately, we don't need to experience the same tragedies as others in order to feel empathy for them. As Troy spoke, I could easily imagine how devastated I would have been had I lost my mother when I was 14. Most of us can readily understand and relate to Troy's grief, as well as the grief of his victim's mother. When we do understand and relate to the pain and sorrow of others, we are empathizing.

Consider the following scenario: You're walking along in your housing unit when suddenly a prisoner storms out of the counselor's office, bumps into you abruptly, and keeps on stepping without saying a word. What would be your initial reaction? Would you curse him out? Would you shout, "Hey, man, why don't you watch where you're going?" Would you go after him?

Or would you take a minute to stop and analyze the situation? You don't really know what took place inside the counselor's office that made the guy react the way he did, do you? Maybe you've even left your counselor's office feeling angry. Say you decide it would be a good idea to give this fellow some time to cool off and then talk with him. When you do, you find out that there was a death in his family and the judge had denied his petition to attend the funeral. By taking the time to *empathize* with this prisoner, you're exercising patience, tolerance, and a caring attitude toward others. In addition, you're becoming a better thinker and less self-centered. That's a lot in return for biting your tongue and exercising a little restraint! When you take the time to talk with this prisoner, he'll probably apologize for bumping into you, and the situation will more than likely be resolved in a positive, peaceful way.

The next time you see someone angry and in need of space, or anxious to be the first to get the telephone, or wearing a scowl when they look your way, stop before you react negatively or pass judgment. Believe me, *you* will be that other person someday, and when you are, you'll want empathy from others. Treat others who are struggling in a way that you would want to be treated.

Likewise, when you're thinking about doing something that may affect another person – e.g., borrowing something from you cellmate without asking, placing a demand on a friend or family member, saying something harsh or disrespectful to someone --, stop and put yourself in their shoes for a minute. Ask yourself how you would feel if what you're about to say or do was done to you. Just think! If we'd learned to practice empathy earlier in our lives, many of us wouldn't have violated the lives and rights of others.

Practice empathy every chance you get. When you do, you'll make your life – and the lives of those around you – a little easier and a lot more positive!

## 22

# TRY A NEW APPROACH

How often do we overreact, lash out in frustration, or respond impulsively to someone – a friend, child, parent, spouse, counselor, cellmate, or guard – and receive, in kind, a response we don't like? Then the next time we're frustrated, we do the same thing and get the same results. You'd think after thousands of attempts, we'd get the message. (But usually we don't.)

Back in the '80s a friend of mine named Jerome was enrolled in an analytical reading course I was teaching. Except for the three to five he was serving for grand theft, Jerome had everything going for him—intelligence, ambition, wit, a yearning for knowledge. Each week, he came to class prepared and eager to lead discussions and debates. After class, he always had thoughtful questions for me to answer on our way back to the cellblock.

When I first met Jerome, he seemed to have only one major flaw: He hated authority. Out of the blue, he would fly into a fit of rage over some really minor thing a guard would say to him. For example, the school officer would tell him to move on when he stopped to talk with the secretary, or the block officer would tell him to "take it in" when he was standing out on the tier in front of his cell, or the dining hall officer would order him to remove his hat, or some other equally harmless part of daily life in prison.

During these incidents, Jerome would ball up his fists, assume an aggressive stance, and get right in the guard's face with a verbal assault. Almost every time, he would wind up getting thirty days in the hole because he went too far with his mouth.

Once, when Jerome came out of the hole after one of these thirty-day stints, he strolled up to me and said, "Damn, they pulled me off my square again."

Jerome was wrong: The guard didn't pull him off his square. He pulled himself off his square. When I asked him why he kept feeding into the guard's actions, he told me that he thought that by intimidating the guards, he could get them off of his back once and for all. It never worked – but he kept trying.

After a while, Jerome came to realize that the problem wasn't the guards, but his own reactions to their behavior. He eventually saw how he was contributing to the problem, and he was able to make some major changes in his attitude and his actions. One day we sat down and talked about what his immediate priorities were – completing as many college courses as he could before he made parole, trying to mend his relationship with his girl, and staying out of the hole.

Jerome gave up his attempts at intimidating guards by reminding himself that his goals meant more to him than getting the last word in and winding up in the hole. He was even able to develop a sense of humor about his "gangsta" reactions. Needless to say, Jerome made his days in prison much easier. (And probably on the streets too. He went home and as of this writing, he hasn't returned!)

To some extent, we all share this problem. Whether it's our typical reaction to criticism, a cynical counselor, the way we fail to listen carefully and instead interrupt other people in mid-sentence, or something else, there's usually some pattern in which we do the same thing over and over and expect a different response.

Here's an example: Almost every week, I used to return from my R&B group rehearsals feeling frustrated and irritable. The reason was always obvious. I had the same expectations each week that everyone would come to rehearsal knowing their parts and ready to play. Rarely did this happen, though. Inevitably, there was always someone who wasn't prepared or on the same page as the rest of the group.

One evening, after a really productive practice session, I returned to my cell feeling elated and wondering why every session couldn't be like the one we'd just had. I started thinking about how each musician had played his part so well on the songs we'd been working on for weeks. Then it came to me – I knew why every session couldn't be like that night's session. Only two of the musicians in the group had their own instruments!

The drummer didn't have drums in his cell, so he couldn't practice all the breaks in the songs. The horn players didn't have horns, and their work schedules didn't allow them to get over to the band room during the day to practice in the practice booths. Only the keyboard player and I had our own instruments. This meant that it would always take us a little longer to get the songs as tight as we wanted them to be.

Realizing all of this helped me to put things in perspective and change my expectations. I've been a lot happier on Tuesday nights ever since.

Can you think of times when you've repeated the same behavior and expected different results each time? If you're in school, maybe you keep getting the same kind of math problem wrong because you haven't taken the time to stop and learn the rule or steps in the process. Or maybe you look up the same word again and again in the dictionary. I used to do this all the time. I'd quickly look up a new word, understand its meaning, and then go right back to reading. Weeks later, I'd come across the same word and grow frustrated because I didn't remember its meaning. That's because I never took the time to *learn* and apply the meaning in the first place.

Here's another example that might be familiar to you. I call it the "2-for-1 phenomenon." Just about every cell block in every prison has a "store man," someone who'll give you one food item for two in return, or two for three. If you patronize these store men, you can't help but remain in debt month after month. Every time you get twenty dollars on the books and go to the commissary, you wind up paying most of it to the store man. You come on the block with a bag full of goodies that belong to the store man and, naturally, you're frustrated.

All you need to do is try a new approach. Sacrifice for a month, pay off your debts, and the next time you go to the store, you can shop entirely for yourself.

Whenever you experience repeated frustration over the same things, you can break the cycle by changing your approach. The first step is to take an inventory of your own habits and tendencies so you can see how you've been contributing to the problem. If you're constantly getting into arguments, for example, you might discover that you've always felt the need to get in the last word. (Which is one sure-fire way to keep an argument going!) Hopefully now, though, you realize that your own peace of mind is more important than winning or prolonging an argument. From now on, whenever you find yourself starting an argument or being lured into one, take care of yourself. You can have the first and last words to yourself in your mind. Tell yourself: "It's not worth it." You might even try injecting a little humor into the situation by telling yourself or the other person, "Sure you're right!" or "My bad!"

Remember, it's always in your own best interest to find out why you're frustrated when you're feeling that way. Only when you see the role you play in your frustrations will you be able to turn the situation into a problem that you can solve using the new skills you're learning. Before you know it, you'll be shouting, either outwardly or within, "Eureka! I've got it!"

# 23

# DEVELOP A SUPPORT TEAM

For several years now, one of my hobbies has been to keep track of each year's best movies and academy award nominees. When the Academy Award Ceremony comes around each year, I make a ritual out of preparing for the evening. I get out my bag of popcorn, make a large mug of iced tea (without the ice, of course), and unfold my ballot sheet.

When the winners are announced, it's inevitable that I find myself saying either, "No way!" or "Yes! I knew it!" My favorite moment of the evening is when some actor or actress leans toward the microphone and, in the midst of exhilaration, says, "I'm truly indebted to my friends and family." (And then the list comes out.) "I want to thank so and so…I wouldn't be what I am today without every one of you."

For me, it's always a humbling experience to witness people giving thanks to others. These testimonies of gratitude remind me just how much we need others in our lives.

There's nothing more important in life than striving to become a better human being. It takes courage and fortitude to wake up every day and recommit to being a better person than you were the day before. It's for these reasons that we need the love and support of others.

The best place to start building a personal support system is with family. If you have parents or siblings or other relatives you were once close with but who aren't presently in your life, there's no better time than now to get in touch with them. If you need to make apologies to some of them, do it. Then share some of the personal changes you've made in your life and how you're taking responsibility for your own happiness and peace of mind. Don't ask for anything except their love. If you don't hear from them right away, keep writing.

If you don't have any family, you still need others in your life. No matter what prison you're in, you'll find others who are doing the same thing with their lives that you're doing with yours. Even if they're not exactly about what you're about, if they're positive thinking and productive people, they are likely to make worthwhile friends. When you find one, cherish him or her like the rare gem they are.

Another integral component of a good support system is a religious or spiritual advisor. If you belong to a traditional religion, you should attend religious services and get involved in your religious community. Get to know your clergy leader. He or she can help you answer questions about your faith and beliefs.

If you're not a part of a traditional religion or not religious at all, you still need *spiritual nourishment*. You can get spiritual nourishment by reading good literature and self-help books and by being around others whose values and life goals are similar to your own.

The saying, "No man is an island," simply means that we need others. We need support for just about anything we do in life. The more people we can turn to for guidance and inspiration, the better off we are. Some of my strongest support and inspiration have come from heroes and role models. Here are just a few of them:

*My late grandfather, Mr. Ernest A. Middleton,* Sr. My grandfather's unconditional love, his words of wisdom in our private conversations, and the memories of all the wonderful times we shared, are with me everyday.

*My childhood best friend, Dan Miller.* Dan and I went to Catholic school together for the first eight years. During that time, we were inseparable. Intellectually superior, Dan always invited me to lean on him for help. He taught me Latin so we could serve Mass together; he brought me to his home for refuge when my own home was in turmoil. Not once did he ever question my delinquent behavior or immature ways. After high school, we lost touch for a long time. Twelve years ago I found Dan and wrote to thank him for his unconditional friendship. Once again, I'm blessed to have my old friend back in my life.

*My undergraduate advisor, Dr. Fiore Pugliano.* From the day we first met, Dr. Pugliano has been a constant source of inspiration and encouragement for me. At a time in my life when I needed intellectual guidance the most, Dr. Pugliano was the man. He has taught me much about loyalty and friendship.

*The author Toni Morrison.* No writer has made me laugh and cry and reflect and appreciate life more than this genius of a woman. The characters in her novels breathe life inside me each time I think of them. Without characters like Cholly and Pecola Breedlove, Milkman Dead, Stamp Paid, Sula Peace, Nel Wright, BoyBoy, Sethe, and Baby Suggs, my life would be less than what it is.

*Dr. Martin Luther King, Jr.* His never-ending forgiveness of others may be the most important lesson he gave us. Dr. King is a hero to me because he died trying to make conditions in the world better for all of us. His ideals were the highest mankind can strive for.

*My sister Suzanne.* Every time I think of all she gives to others, to her community, to her family and friends, I feel honored and blessed to have her in my life. She is my role model because she doesn't just talk the talk – she walks the walk.

It is through these people and others that I've been able to develop and confirm my own ideals and values and to strive to become a better human being.

If you take some time to stop and reflect, you'll probably realize that you already have a few role models in your life – people whose qualities you admire and wish to emulate. These individuals are a part of your support team. You need others, too – friends and family members – to love you and encourage you as you continue on your journey to becoming a healthy, responsible person. Search them out. Be patient. They'll come to you. When they do, be ready to nurture each and every one of them.

# 24

# CONNECT WITH YOUR CHILD

If you have a child or children that you've been out of contact with during your incarceration, or even before, you've probably told yourself at one time or another that your child is better off without you. Perhaps you've even been told that your child doesn't want to have anything to do with you. If you grew up without one or both of your parents in your life, you probably know this isn't true. The fact is, children want their mothers and fathers in their lives, in some form or fashion, no matter how much time has gone by without them.

Unless you committed a crime against your child, you have an obligation to try and reconnect with him or her no matter what you think the outcome might be.

There are some important things you need to know, though, before you attempt to make contact with your child. First, prepare yourself for a less-than-positive initial response. Depending on the circumstances, your child might be very angry, and he or she might want to tell you a thing or two about it! This is quite normal. You need to allow your child that anger, no matter how difficult it is to hear it.

When my own father got in touch with me after being absent from my life for seventeen years, it was a stormy journey for both of us at first. I had a large wall of anger built up inside of me. Fortunately, my father handled all of my hurtful words and humiliation with grace and patience. Together, we chipped away at that wall and built a loving and healthy relationship.

Before you make the decision to reconnect with your child, I urge you to ask yourself a very important question: Am I willing to stick with this even if all I get in return is anger and silence? It may take years of sending unanswered cards and letters. Are you willing to keep trying?

The idea of having to be patient, possibly for years, can be discouraging, but don't give up before you even begin. This is your child! Trust doesn't come easy. Years of hurt can't be undone overnight. You're going to have to show your child – perhaps for the very first time – that you can be trusted; that you are committed to being a permanent presence in his or her life. You will have to show your child that you aren't afraid to apologize for your mistakes as a parent. Wouldn't you have wanted the same thing from your parent(s)?

Once you've prepared yourself emotionally for what may come and you've made the commitment to stick it out, you're ready to make your first contact. Now your work really begins! Even if your child welcomes you into his or her life from the start, it's going to take time to build the foundation for a solid relationship. The primary problem you'll have to contend with is that of having little or no history with your child. If you have no stories or memories to share, things might feel extremely awkward until you are able to build some history together through letters, cards, phone calls, gifts, and, if possible, face to face visits. Only then will the relationship with your child begin to truly develop.

If your initial contact brings only silence, it's normal to feel discouraged, but don't give up! Remember that trust isn't built overnight. This, believe it or not, is the time when you need to remain consistent and patient and keep writing. Hang in there! Your child will notice your commitment, and it will help to build your relationship.

Waiting for a response from your child can feel like slow torture, but there are some things you can do to pass that time constructively. For example, you can start a journal. Write a couple of lines each day telling your child about yourself, your memories, your family's history (which is also your child's history), and the hopes and dreams you have for the two of you. The day may arrive when you can share your journal, because your child may decide it's time to go look for dad!

In prisons all over the world, fathers are taking the necessary steps every day to reclaim their children. Just recently, a friend of mine was blessed with a letter and school picture from his 9-year-old son whom he hadn't seen or heard from in five years. The two of them have been writing, sharing pictures, and catching up on their lives. Another dad I know found his daughter after sixteen years of separation. The first few visits were filled with emotions and much joy, but then the relationship hit the difficult "building phase" that is so familiar to long-distance parents.

A few words of caution: Trying to reconnect with your children doesn't always work. Many fathers who try to reconnect with their children are successful; others are not. To make it work, it will take *both* of you. Also, keep in mind that your child may want to have contact with you, but not at the same deep level you'd like.

Some moms and dads are able to build very close relationships with their children; others only get cards for holidays and birthdays and a visit once or twice a year. But even these moms and dads, if you ask them, will tell you that what they have now is better than no connection at all.

Then there are moms and dads who, unfortunately, can't locate their children or have their cards and letters intercepted by angry family members. If this happens to you, don't give up! Someday your child will be an adult who is free to make his or her own decisions. Someday your grown child might be surprised to find out that you tried to find them all those years ago. Never lose hope.

So now it's time to send that card or make that call. Take it slowly. Don't overwhelm your child with your whole life story in your first letter or phone call. Just make that initial connection. With patience, commitment and love, you'll have your whole life to share with your child.

# 25

# ACKNOWLEDGE YOUR SUCCESS

Not long ago on a Tuesday afternoon, my friend Cheryl was in her office at the university where she works. The director of another unit stopped by and asked Cheryl if she had a few minutes to talk. Cheryl had interviewed a few weeks prior for a job in the director's unit, and Cheryl was sure that the director was coming to tell her that the search committee had finally made a decision. She was right – not only had the search committee made a decision, but they had unanimously decided to offer Cheryl the job! This would be a big promotion for her, and she was ecstatic.

When Cheryl shared the news with me on the phone that evening, I asked her what she was going to do to celebrate. First, she chuckled and then she replied, "I hadn't really thought about celebrating, but I like the idea. Maybe I'll buy a new CD."

At work the next day, friends and colleagues found their way into Cheryl's office one by one to congratulate her. One of her closest friends stopped by to announce that she was planning a Sunday afternoon cookout to celebrate Cheryl's new job. Cheryl felt deeply honored and somewhat overwhelmed.

When people set real goals for themselves and work hard to achieve them, it's nice to have their successes acknowledged by family and friends. Such acknowledgements inspire us and often reaffirm our own feelings that what we've accomplished is worthwhile and important. This, in turn, gives an often-needed boost to our self-esteem.

No matter how loving and caring our friends are, though, we can't always expect them to celebrate each and every little success we enjoy in life. Nor should we want them to!

If one of your goals is to be kinder and more patient with others, for example, it wouldn't be very appropriate to have a friend pat you on the back and say, "Way to go!" every time you refrain from being rude to someone. Or, say your goal is to watch less television and use the time to study for your GED, vocational, or college classes (or the exercises in this book). After a month goes by, you look back and see that you've used the time well. You're pleased with the discipline you've acquired, so you pump your fists in the air.

You should be proud, for not only have you increased your study time (which will pay dividends later), but you've also increased your willpower.

Both of the above examples involve the kind of personal success that usually doesn't get noticed by our friends. But that doesn't mean they shouldn't be acknowledged. *Every* step of progress you make in your daily journey toward personal growth and development is a success, and you should recognize each one and give yourself credit.

Have you ever witnessed a parent helping her child learn how to walk? Perhaps you've taken part in this precious experience. Each time the child begins to fall, the parent is there to catch her. And each time the child takes a successful step forward, the parent praises and encourages her.

Hopefully, you're learning new skills every day. You're learning how to walk with honesty and discipline and integrity and persistence! And much of this learning you must do alone in the solitude of your inner world. It's critical that you learn how to nurture yourself in this life-long process. Here are some tips to help you along the way.

*Make rewards appropriate.* Keep your rewards in proportion to the size of your goal. For example, if you've spent a year studying every day for the GED test and then you take the test and pass it, you need to acknowledge your success big time! If you're trying to reduce smoking from a pack a day to a half pack a day, and you're successful for the first couple of days, a simple self-acknowledgement is appropriate. When you've stopped smoking altogether for a week, that's when you need to take out the chocolate bar or bag of party mix that you've stashed away and get busy!

*Be creative!* Rewards don't always have to be tangible ones. You can reward yourself simply by reminding yourself each time you succeed that you're winning. If you like poetry or paintings, have a book of your favorite poetry or paintings around to look at when you've just achieved a small goal.

Perhaps you've always wanted to start a hobby (e.g., learning about the personal lives of your favorite athletes or singers, collecting stamps, drawing, writing). Use the successful completion of a major goal to begin your hobby. Sometimes after completing a goal, I'll reward myself by doing something for someone else. By doing so, I fulfill another goal – to help others whenever I can.

*Be consistent.* Progress in reaching some goals is so often subtle, and the gains are sometimes difficult to measure. No one but you can monitor your progress. That's why it's important to make sure your goals are clear to you.

*Specify your rewards.* When writing out your goals, decide how you're going to reward yourself once you've completed a particular goal, and write that reward down. Examples:

*Goal:* To spend one hour every weeknight reading and studying.
*Reward:* After successfully completing this goal for two weeks, I'll reward myself with an ice cream (or a soda, or a late-night movie) on Saturday or Sunday. After successfully completing this goal for an entire month, I'll share the news with family members and spend the next weekend in the yard with friends.

*Goal:* To refrain from contributing hateful or negative comments toward others during conversations with peers.
*Reward:* Each time I successfully keep my thoughts and tongue in check, I'll remind myself that the more I gain control over this undesirable behavior, the better I'm going

to feel about myself. After a month of success, I'll tell at least one person that I associate with and who engages in this behavior that I don't have time for talking trash about others.

I find it helpful to ask the question: How will I know when I'm making progress on a goal, or when I've successfully completed a specific goal?

If you start each day with an inventory of what your major short-term and long-term goals are, you're better able to monitor your progress and acknowledge your success throughout each day.

When you find that you've let days go by without monitoring your progress, don't sweat it. Start over again, and again and again if you have to, until you've made this a new habit. Consistency is the key to success. Acknowledge it!

## 26

# OPEN YOUR COCOON

A friend of mine named Brenda is married to a prisoner who was recently transferred from a jail near their home to a new facility halfway across the state. What had once been a one-hour round-trip drive for her and their young daughter was now a four-hour drive one-way. Brenda works long hours during the week to support their family, yet she always wakes at 4:00 a.m. on Saturdays to make the trip to see her husband.

One Friday morning, Brenda awoke feeling sick. She went to work, but the longer the day went on, the worse she felt. She was sure she was coming down with the same flu that many of her co-workers were battling. By the time she arrived home that night, she had a fever, a pounding headache, and felt like she could sleep for days.

When Brenda's husband called later that evening, Brenda described how badly she was feeling and asked if he would mind if they postponed their visit the next day. Her husband got angry. "What am I supposed to do tomorrow?" he yelled. "Is it so bad that you can't drive up here with my daughter?" At 4:00 the next morning, Brenda got herself out of bed, dressed their daughter, and started the long drive to the prison.

Now, no one can fault Brenda's husband for missing his family and wanting to be with them. Their Saturday visits helped to sustain him throughout the rest of the week. But, in this situation, he was obviously not taking very good care of his family. Here was an opportunity for him to make his wife Brenda feel valued, but he was thinking only about himself.

In an earlier chapter, I talked about the cocoons people sometimes build around themselves in order to survive. While this *coping strategy* isn't unique to people in prison, it is a common tool we prisoners use to protect ourselves (often without ever realizing it). Building a cocoon – some call it a "wall" – helps keep out anything that threatens us physically or hurts us emotionally. It allows us to appear in control, *cool*, most of the time. A prisoner whose family didn't visit on Christmas might say to himself: *"Who cares? It's just a stupid, overblown, commercialized rip-off holiday in the first place."* Another whose girlfriend stopped accepting his phone calls might think: *"Hell, I've got nothing to say to her anyway."*

Living in a cocoon allows you to create a world in which you call the shots. Your comfort and happiness are always priority number one. There's no fear, no pain, no embarrassment, no loneliness and, as a result, no (or very little) reality. That's because living in a cocoon prevents you from seeing very far beyond yourself. And if you want to have a healthy, long-lasting marriage in or out of prison, you have to build a cocoon big enough for two people – even bigger if you have children.

The cocoon Brenda's husband built around himself prevented him from seeing anything other than his own needs. It wasn't open enough to hear the weakness in Brenda's voice the night she was sick, when she asked to postpone their visit. It prevented him, too, from recognizing how exhausted and pale Brenda was when she finally arrived at the prison that Saturday. The cocoon Brenda's husband built was only big enough for himself.

Can you think of a time when you put your needs above those of your wife, husband, child(ren), mother, father, etc.? We've all done it at one time or another. The trouble starts when our needs always have to come first. If Brenda's husband keeps expecting her to make eight-hour round-trip drives when she's sick, it won't be long before Brenda stops visiting altogether. Just think if he'd said, "Honey, for the last three months you've been working like a dog all week and then coming to see me every Saturday. I miss you like crazy, but our visit can wait until next week. Stay home tomorrow and get some rest."

In those three short sentences, Brenda's husband would have honored the work Brenda puts into supporting their marriage; reassured Brenda that he loves and misses her; and shown Brenda that her health and well-being are important to him.

Just because you're in prison doesn't mean you can't help your loved ones at home. You may be limited in how you can help, but you can always do something. Letters, poems, and artwork are great places to start. You can also show patience, compassion, and understanding for what they may be going through in their lives. As an exercise, spend the next phone call with your spouse, parent, or friend talking only about *them*. Ask how their week is going? Ask what new things have happened since you last talked. Talk about their hobbies and interests. It might even be fun to ask a question like, "If you could be any one person for a day, who would you be?" This might feel awkward at first – for both of you, but over time *actively listening* to the people you love most will only help to strengthen your connection with them. It will also show them that you truly love and value them, and that is perhaps the most precious gift you will ever send home.

# 27

# KICK GOSSIP TO THE CURB

How many hurt feelings, broken friendships, and damaged relationships could be avoided were it not for gossip and rumor mills? And how many real possibilities for good things in life have been wiped out by gossip?

The type of gossip I'm referring to isn't the kind like, "Did you hear they're going to stop selling squeeze bottles in the commissary?" or "Jamaal says he's not interested in seeing his ex-girlfriend, but I think he'd jump through hoops if she showed up for a visit." Remarks like these do no harm. But there are plenty of others that do.

Back in the early '80s, a good friend of mine returned to prison after being out on parole for about a year. Wayne had been one of the best athletes in the prison. He was intelligent, tough, witty, and popular with everyone in the joint. Every week, family, friends, and girlfriends came to see him. That's how we all remembered him.

When Wayne returned to prison, we hardly recognized him. He was as thin as a rail, very pale, and his hair was falling out. It was obvious that he was very sick.

Almost immediately, the rumors began to fly that Wayne was dying of AIDS.

Sadly, not one of Wayne's friends – myself included – bothered to ask Wayne about the true nature of his illness. As the gossip circulated that he had AIDS, the details grew more elaborate about how he'd contracted the disease, which seemed to add credibility to the story.

Wayne had always been a player with the ladies. Some said he'd been hanging out with prostitutes and had probably been infected by one of them. Others said he'd started shooting heroin again and had gotten AIDS from a dirty needle. This was the mid-eighties and we knew very little about AIDS other than that it was a deadly disease. There was still much speculation over how the disease could be passed on to others. Consequently, we were all reluctant to even be around Wayne.

Eventually, Wayne became too weak to remain in the general population and was admitted to the prison hospital, much – I'm ashamed to say – to his friends' relief.

When Wayne died later that summer, the local newspaper revealed that he'd died of cancer. He never had AIDS! Those of us who called ourselves his "friends" were too embarrassed to even talk about how foolish we'd been. Every one of us were guilty of taking part in the rumors and gossip that led to his being ostracized. We'd let our friend spend his last days alone. Had we simply taken the time to inquire about his illness, we would have learned the truth. We would have been able to show him love and support while he was still with us. All of us had let Wayne down.

It doesn't take a scientific study to know that there's a strong relationship between a person's self-esteem and the degree to which a person gossips. In general, the more self-esteem we have, the less we engage in gossip and rumor spreading. As you continue to mature and rid yourself of unhealthy habits, you may want to ask yourself if you're taking part in destructive gossip. If you are, there are ways to stop.

First, consider the most common reason why people gossip. It gives us a feeling of power and control, of being in charge. Having the "scoop" on someone and then sharing it with others makes us feel like we have a certain amount of status.

There's nothing wrong with wanting to gain respectable status or wanting to feel in control of our lives. But gossip isn't the way to get it. You already know other ways to satisfy the need for those feelings – through genuine accomplishments. You're discovering ways to feel good about yourself all by yourself – not by exercising power over others through gossip.

Second, think about covering your own back. You can't hang with people who routinely gossip and actually believe that you're never the subject of their gossip when you're not around! If the people you hang out with are into talking about other people behind their backs, what reason do you have to think that you won't be next? Choose your company wisely!

Third, put a piece of gossip through a four-way test. If it flunks any part, you should keep whatever it is to yourself or find a different way of saying it. Ask yourself the following questions:

1) *Is it true?* If you don't know for sure that what you're about to say is 100% true, you shouldn't say it. There are exceptions to this rule. When you're trying to help someone, for example – a friend is talking about suicide, and you want to tell someone who can take action. This is not gossip.

2) *Is it necessary?* Even if you know something is true, ask yourself if it's really necessary to repeat it to others. *Necessary* is the key word here. If you know something will likely cause harm to someone and you can prevent the harm by speaking up, then it's necessary to say what you know.

3) *Is it mean-spirited?* Say the rumor is true, and it's even necessary to repeat. Is the way you're going to say it kind, or will it be more like a personal attack? Keep your tone respectful at all times.

4) *Would you still say it if you knew that person only had a couple of weeks left to live?* Or would you say it if you knew the person's mother or father had just died?

Asking yourself such questions may humble you and enable you to realize that you wouldn't want to cause further pain to someone. So why say what you're thinking about saying and cause pain now?

Finally, it helps to remember that people don't carry tales where there are no ears to listen to them. You can let it be known discreetly, through your actions as well as your words, that you don't feed into gossip. Maybe your friends will follow your example. It could stop a lot of grief and wasted time – and the reputation you save may be your own.

# 28

# LIVE EVERY DAY WITH A PURPOSE

Nothing keeps us shackled to the chains of boredom and misery more than a lack of purpose.

If we were to examine a typical day in the life of any one of us prisoners, we'd find very little cliff-hanging, bungee jumping, speeding-down-the-highway-to-destination-anywhere excitement. Our environment restricts us from such activities. It doesn't restrict us, though, from living with a purpose and finding meaning and contentment in the things we can do for ourselves.

I'll never forget how my life changed after I met a small group of prisoners called the "frat boys." The frat boys were five students in the University of Pittsburgh's prison college program. It was the summer of 1979, and I was in my first semester of studies when they invited me to sit alongside them on the top row of bleachers in the prison courtyard.

The first day they were sharing sections of the newspaper and discussing the medieval imagination. I was immediately impressed by the way they carried themselves. When one of them mentioned that he had an exam the following week, another began priming him for it. A third one was the coordinator of a Scared Straight program for juveniles and asked who wanted to come to the next session and talk with the kids. When I glanced curiously at this fellow, he asked if I would be interested in sharing my story with the group who was coming for a visit from a nearby youth development center. I told him I was.

The frat boys didn't seem to be bothered by the fact that they were doing time in prison. They were too busy meeting goals and leading productive lives to waste time dwelling on where they were living. These men were living each day with a purpose!

The frat boys demonstrated an important lesson to me. As I observed them over the weeks and months, I saw how they played sports and music, headed prisoner organizations, ran departments, and interacted with other prisoners in a positive, exemplary manner. They had fun, they laughed and joked, they maintained their composure, and they were always focused on a goal. The frat boys were living examples that it's not *what* we do, but rather *how* we do what we do. When you're at work or in school, or you're playing a game of handball or basketball, or just sitting outside on the bleachers (alone or with others), you can still laugh and have fun and at the same time live with a purpose. Wherever you're at and whatever you're doing, you can always stay focused on your higher goals. You can, for example:

1. refrain from talking negatively about others
2. remain vigilant over your thoughts
3. observe your behavior and the behavior of those around you
4. practice living in the present moment
5. set positive examples of appropriate behavior to others
6. practice being calm and at peace
7. maintain your dignity and self-respect
8. check in with yourself from time to time to acknowledge that you're okay and that you're taking care of yourself.

(These examples are only the beginning. Your own list will no doubt include these and other purposes.)

The more you practice living with a purpose, the more you'll begin to notice and appreciate the role you play in your own happiness. Only you can bring about the changes you want to make in your life. You've already established meaningful short-term and long-term goals. Now keep your eyes, heart, and spirit focused on seeing each one of them through.

Remember that your peace of mind and well-being come down to one thing – how you look at life. If you renew your commitments each day, you'll be living with a purpose. And that's what life's about!

## 29

# DISCOVER THE UNIVERSAL TRUTH

If I had a nickel for every time I read something that caused me to exclaim, "How did the author know that?" or "I knew it all the time!" or "This author's gotta stop renting space in my head!", I'd have enough coins to fill several large piggy banks. Seriously, how many time have you read something in a magazine article or in a book that confirmed your own ideas and thoughts? For me, these are some of life's greatest moments.

Ralph Waldo Emerson described this phenomenon perfectly when he wrote: "Tomorrow a stranger will say with masterly good sense precisely what we have thought and felt all the time."

When I was in college, I started transcribing my favorite quotes and passages in a journal that I titled *Universal Truths*. My first entry in the journal came from a letter written by the great Russian writer Fyodor Dostoyevsky. Dostoyevsky had been sent to prison camp in Siberia for speaking out against the Czar. While there, he wrote to his brother Mikhail about his condition: "My brother, I do not despair. I am not dejected. For I have found that life is life everywhere; life is in ourselves, not in the world that surrounds us."

When I first read these words, I was overcome with joy and awe, for there was something strikingly familiar about them. This *universal truth* had been speaking to me for some time. *"Life is in ourselves, not in the world that surrounds us."* These words brought an epiphany to me. I discovered there was another world apart from the material world, and it was beckoning me to explore it!

As you continue to explore your own inner world, you can find an infinite source of solace, guidance, and instruction by reading good literature – poetry, novels, plays, philosophy, and other self-help books. Whenever you read something that stirs your heart and mind, I urge you to write it down and keep it forever. There will be times when you need inspiration, when you lose your way, or when you just want to look back and see how deeply you've nourished yourself and how far you've come. When these moments occur, you'll be grateful that these affirmations are there for you.

Here are some of my favorite quotes and passages that I have collected over the past twenty years.

"Though we should soar into the heavens, though we should sink into the abyss, we never go out of ourselves, it is always our own thoughts we perceive."

– Ralph Waldo Emerson

"The most important thing about 'vision' is the precise knowledge of what you are trying to achieve."
—Colin Wilson

"Those who do not succeed fail because they are lazy."
– Albert Camus

"Every human [being] that does not know itself as spirit is in despair. And what is even more important, a man who is in despair need not know that he is. He may think himself perfectly happy."
– Soren Kierkegaard

"Highly intentional mental activity, like highly intentional physical activity, produces a feeling of power and strength, of self-control, of vitality."
– Husserl

"Our energies are almost infinite; but when there is no challenge, no threat present, we tend to fall into a state of *sleep*. And in sleep, the robot takes over; it is a kind of vicious cycle."
– Colin Wilson

"Our eyes are beholden that we cannot see things that stare us in the face, until the hour arrives when the mind is ripened; then we behold them, and the time when we saw them not is like a dream."
– Ralph Waldo Emerson

"There is nothing noble in being superior to some other man. The true nobility is in being superior to your previous self."
— Hindu Proverb

"No man can produce great things who is not thoroughly sincere in dealing with himself."
— James Russell Lowell

The great virtue in man lies in his ability to correct his mistakes and continually to make a new man of himself."
— Wang Yang-Ming

"When a man's fight begins with himself, he is worth something."
— Robert Browing

"All that we are is the result of what we have thought. The mind is everything. What we think, we become."
— Buddha

"The brain will not fail when the will is in earnest."
— George Bernard Shaw

"To be free is nothing; to become free is very heaven."
— Johann Fichte

"All men have my blood, and I have all men's."
— Ralph Waldo Emerson

"Happiness is the feeling that obstacles are being overcome, that you are conquering."
— Friedrich Nietzsche

"For the thinker, as for the artist, what counts in life is not the number of rare and exciting adventures a man encounters, but the inner depth of that life."
— William Barrett

"Don't be discouraged because the way of consciousness is difficult. Press on, and you will find that it will be more worthwhile than you can ever imagine."
— William James

"Freedom is not simply being allowed to do what you like; it is intensity of will, and it appears under any circumstances that limit man and arouse his will to more life."
— Colin Wilson

"Emancipation from error is real knowledge."
— Anonymous

"The thing to understand is that most of our suffering in life can ultimately be traced to what may be called alienation from the self."
— Obadiah Silas Harris

"We talk of freedom with great passion, but actually we try to escape from freedom because freedom imposes responsibility."

– Erich Fromm

"A man or woman becomes fully human only by his or her choices and his or her commitments. Real worth and dignity is attained by the multitude of decisions we make from day to day. These decisions require courage."

– Rollo May

"The great thing about life is that as long as we live we have the privilege of growing."

– Author Unknown

"There is only one way to happiness, and that is to cease worrying about things which are beyond the power of our will."

– Epictetus

"The lesson which these observations convey is, Be, and not seem."

– Ralph Waldo Emerson

Patrick Middleton, Ph.D. Prisoner #AK-3703 1975-

# ABOUT THE AUTHOR

In 1990, author Patrick Middleton became the first prisoner in America to earn his Bachelor of Arts, Master's and Ph.D. degrees, all while incarcerated. His academic accomplishments were made possible through the University of Pittsburgh. During his tenure as a graduate student, he taught and lectured undergraduates; paid room and board to the Department of Corrections; won several fellowships, teaching awards, and small literary prizes; and co-authored a textbook in experimental psychology with the University's Dean of Psychology.

Today, 29 years into his incarceration, he is working on the final chapters of his autobiography, tentatively titled, *I Shade My Laurels: The Autobiography of An American Criminal*.

# SELECTED POEMS

**HOPE IS A ROSE**

Prison is a barren land.
The earth – a fertile Thief—
sprouts—I'm told—
a withering rose.

Subjectivity has its foibles though,
the Eye's bramble –
For—in my narrow plot—
The Rose – How it grows!
How it grows!

**SERENDIPITY**

Among the clamorous crowd
of angry men,
I saw seven shining
birds gather
in a choir
on rows
of rusted barbed-wire.

Elated for the moment,
I discerned,
beyond the scene,
the absence
of ball and chain.

## IT'S SUMMER AND

this prison is
alive again
if you pay
attention to
the way it
breathes
it won't hurt
you but you
have to
take some
precautions


like minding
your own
bizness
and looking
straight ahead.


It's summer and
the yard is
one big neighborhood
of cliques
some say
cliques are

as necessary
as knives
here
I say
be your
own
clique.


I say too
it's not
all bad
here.


It's summer and
God had blessed
us with
the scent of
fresh-cut grass
the rhythm of
blue rubber balls
bouncing against
the wall
an evening sky
speckled with
blackbirds and
blossoms on
an old convict's
flowers.

It's summer and
life goes
on inside this prison
on inside
every man
so I say
be all you can
be inside
be free.